This book should be returned to any branch of the Lancashire County Library on or before the date shown

SANDMAN

THE AUTOBIOGRAPHY OF

CEDRIC ROBINSON

QUEEN'S GUIDE TO THE SANDS

GREAT NORTHERN

Great Northern Books Limited
PO Box 213, Ilkley, LS29 9WS
www.greatnorthernbooks.co.uk

ISBN: 978 1 905080 62 5

Design and layout: David Burrill

CIP Data
A catalogue for this book is available from the British Library

Contents

CHAPTER ONE

Childhood in Flookburgh

THE VILLAGE OF FLOOKBURGH on the West Coast of the Cartmel Peninsula is where my sister Jean and I were born. It was at number 4 Market Cross, and although my father had lived in two different houses in the village, he himself had been born in this very same house back in 1904. Our neighbours, in all the six cottages, were lovely, homely and very friendly people.

At number 1 came Lily and Fred Preston and their daughter Vera, who was about my age. Next door to them was Tom Wilson senior, a fisherman, who lived there with his wife and daughter Ethel, who followed the sands with her father. Elsie and Johnny Wright lived next door to us with their son Billy and daughters Dinah and Kathleen, and then came Nannie Stephenson and her husband Freddie and their son Clem. At the end of the row lived Tom Wilson Junior, his wife Flora and their two children, Roy and Beryl. Roy was my best friend.

It can't have been easy for my mother to cope with us youngsters and a dog and a cat in such a small cottage without any modern conveniences. The rooms were very small, with just a living room and a tiny kitchen downstairs and two tiny bedrooms upstairs but mother always kept the house beautifully clean and tidy.

There were no carpets in those days – just linoleum and coconut matting on the floors. The table was covered with an oilcloth. Nearly every household had the same, but when mother knew of someone visiting us, she would change this and put on a tablecloth made of red chenille which came well down over the sides.

In 1937 aged four I started at the village primary school which was only a short distance from our cottage. The very first day I did not like it at all and at playtime I ran home. The teacher came and found me hiding under the kitchen table, with the tablecloth pulled well down over the sides so I could not be seen. She found me and dragged me out, spanking me as she carried me back to school like a sack of potatoes. Seemingly, I did this on more than one occasion. But despite this very bad start, I did come to like school more and I became a favourite of hers too! But my favourite, at school, was the huge rocking horse we had there and I loved being pampered and put to bed for an hour or so in the afternoons.

I remember coming home from school on a cold wet day to a cosy room with a big red fire and mother making us toast on a long toasting fork with a nice hot steamy cup of cocoa each. We then would play dominoes and ludo with my sister Jean.

We, like most families, had a big galvanised tin bathtub, which was brought into the house from the washhouse outside on bath night. The water was brought into the house in buckets and kettles and heated over the fire. A bucket of clean water always stood on a table in the back kitchen. Dad always shaved with soap and a cut-throat razor and he had a strap hanging from the wall which he used to sharpen his razor on.

Cottages at Market Cross, Flookburgh, drawn specially for this book by my wife Olive. I was born in number 4 in 1933; it had just a living room, kitchen, two tiny bedrooms and no modern conveniences.

The rent mother paid for the cottage was five shillings (25p) a week. This was paid to the landlord who called every week and ticked off the payments in the rent book.

I loved animals and really enjoyed going for walks with my sister Jean and my dog Crackers. We would walk for miles, down to Humphrey Head and Roughem, Sandgate on the Flookburgh shore and down Shore Lane, Green Lane, Moor Lane, Tuet Lane and Ikky Pickie. As long as I was walking I was as happy as a sandboy.

I also had a black and white cat for fourteen years. It went missing for a week and we were really worried about it. About a week later it turned up, as thin as a lath with a rabbit snare tight around its tummy. It soon got well again and all the dogs in our area of Flookbugh Square would give it a wide berth. It was the Boss.

A potter, with his dog, once came to the end of our back yard whilst I was sat on the backdoor step with my cat. I said to him "I wouldn't bring your dog past my cat if I were you." He just laughed at me.

But I was right. The cat jumped on the dog's back and stuck her claws in. The dog screamed with fright and couldn't get away fast enough. The potter couldn't believe his own eyes. He thought he knew better than to take notice of me – me being so young! I never saw the man or his dog again. Well, as the saying goes, 'you're never too old to learn'.

I was given a big white beautiful angora rabbit and spent a full day making a rabbit hutch for it. This was up from the ground on a sturdy frame and I was given hay and some wood shavings for bedding. It stood near the back door of our cottage.

The next morning I got up to find white fluff all over the back yard. Being an open yard, anything could have got to it, but the wire netting was pulled away from the frame so it was thought that this was done by a fox rather than someone's cat.

This did upset me, but moving on, me and my friend Bobby Jarvis, from the Hope and Anchor public house just opposite our cottage acquired a goat from a woman in Cartmel. We used to take it for walks, and even made a small cart – a bogey on wheels with shafts, and yoked it up and pretended we were going out fishing. We'd had a very wet spell of weather and just down the mile road there was a field on the left which was standing in water. We were so excited as we yoked up the goat and led it down Moor Lane and into the field. We, as two young lads, did not know that it was a well known fact that goats do not take easily to water. We managed then to do the impossible, because we succeeded in getting her in almost as deep as we could wade, almost to the top of our wellies. Then we put a long rope to the halter to see if she would go in deeper. She did, and now we were so happy and laughing. We now pretended to be like the Flookburgh fishermen, trawling for shrimps, just like my father.

After some time, we had an idea to breed from our own goat, so we took it back to the person we had bought it from – to get it served with her billy goat. It was there for a week and she charged us for its keep, and the use of her billy. We walked her home and waited patiently – but she never did have a kid, so we went back to see the woman and to get our money back but she wouldn't give it to us.

A short distance from the village, down Moor Lane to the right, led you to Harold Edgar's farm. My sister Jean and I always took a milk can with a lid when we were going blackberrying This was a good place to gather blackberries – in the hedgerows of the farm belonging to Mr Whiteman. We had to pass this very old house which was now empty, but we thought it was haunted and very scary, so we always ran past.

In a field at the end of this lane, there was an old stagnant pond with a small haystack. We loved going into this field because of the big juicy blackberries. We could fill the milk can in a very short time, but we also found a hen's nest full of eggs, so every few days we took the eggs away, leaving one there so that the hen or hens would come back and lay some more.

We thought at the time that they didn't belong to anyone because it was so far away from the farm, and in our minds, if we left them they would just go bad. We also used to go through the field where they now have the Willow Water establishment – a plant where the water is pumped up from the ground, then bottled and sold countrywide. The land around had poor drainage and the hedgerows were mostly of willow.

Jean always liked to take wild flowers back for mum, so we picked a large bunch of pussy willow and lots of the bright yellow flowers called watergallens.

In a paddock just before Harold Edgar's farm was a big walnut tree. To get to it from the road we had to climb a big high wall and this is where we saw this huge bull in the field where we were to gather the walnuts. I climbed up and threw the walnuts down to Jean, who not only had to keep an eye on the bull, but also to keep a lookout for the farmer Harold, who had chased us away before on more than one occasion. When we got home if it was teatime, mum would ask us to go down to the farm for a can of blue milk. That's the milk that has been separated from the cream. We were both nervous waiting for the milk in case Harold served us, but it always seemed to be his wife Jenny who ladled the milk from the churn in the dairy, which at that time was part of the farmhouse and she never ever mentioned anything about the walnuts.

Another very good place was in Holker Park. There was a huge walnut tree right in front of Holker Hall. I took my sister Jean on the crossbar of dad's old bicycle and we were in luck as there were loads of walnuts lying all over the

Flookburgh village, seen from Humphrey Head. (Peter Cherry)

ground. We thought to ourselves we had just timed this right, with no need to climb up the tree at all. We began to fill all of our pockets and then stuffed them down the front of our jumpers, then somehow managed to climb on the bike and set off through the park for home.

We suddenly spotted Lord Richard Cavendish riding a great big horse and galloping after us, and although I peddled like mad, he soon caught up with us and asked us to get off our bike. We stood there scared stiff but he smiled at us and said, "You know you are not supposed to ride bicycles in the park – just walk the rest of the way – now carry on." He never mentioned the walnuts and we heaved a sigh of relief. Looking back he must have noticed we had something stuffed down our jumpers. He was the father of the present Lord Hugh Cavendish. They are a lovely family and very friendly with the local people.

The village of Flookburgh was a well-knit community with all families knowing each other. No one ever seemed to move out of the village and very rarely did anyone move in. Sons often followed their fathers and grandfathers into fishing the Bay for their livelihoods. Increasing numbers on the sands and fishing grounds made the job quite competitive, with some families not speaking to others over feuds on the Bay.

There were very few cars on the roads and no street lighting in the village but it was something to see up to twenty or more fishermen with their horses and carts setting out from Flookburgh. They made their way down Main Street and through the square and then on down the mile long straight road (named The Mile Road) across the marsh and out onto the sands, according to the tides, day and night.

About this time transport was mostly by horse and cart and most businesses were based in the village. There were two coal merchants, George Golding in the Main Street and Macareths down the bottom of Market Street. My dad's sister Auntie Marie owned the grocery and sweet shop in Main Street. Elaine Hodgson had the corner shop in the square for years and her brother John was a fisherman in the Bay. Neither of them ever married.

There was a chemist shop in the Square and Miss Slater and her sister ran the Post Office and wool shop down Market Street. There was a butcher's nearby and a bakery just out of the village over the railway bridge at Piggy Town. This was Hugh's bakery and in later years, his daughter Pat and her husband kept the business going until their retirement. Their meat and potato pies and hot cross buns were a speciality – not to be beaten.

We had a chippie and a cooperative, both now modernised into accommodation. There was a blacksmith's shop, which did a good trade with all the fishermen and farmers with their horses and metal work. Next to the blacksmith's was a cobbler called Mr Jeffries and his son Alan; they also made clogs to order.

Jack Nichols owned a very busy garage and taxi service. He sold bicycles and all the accessories and also repaired them. Two petrol pumps stood outside; one old fashioned pump was hand-operated with a handle, the other slightly more modern. There was opposition, as a second garage stood near to the Cark & Cartmel railway station and was owned and run by a Mr Halsall, his son Harry and daughter Margaret. Both these premises have now been developed into housing.

If you needed a doctor, there were two surgeries at Cark – Dr Charlton and Dr Anderton.

One year we had very deep snow and most families made their own sledges. We took our sledge to Jack Nichols' garage and asked him if he had anything that would make runners for it. Jack was a very obliging chap and if he could help you out in any way he would give it a try. He made us, and fitted, metal runners on our sledge from bits from old bicycle frames and it was so successful that nearly everyone else took their sledges to Jack.

The snow seemed to last for weeks and we sledged down Sandgate Hill on the main road as the only traffic ever seen using the hill in those days was the fishermen's horses and carts. Once the roads cleared we took to the fields, one at the top of Sandgate Hill which the villagers called the heights, and at the other end of the village down Market Street we would trudge through Piggy Town. I never knew how this name came about for this small area of houses. However our destination was in a field at Jack Satts, short for Satterthwaite, at Applebury Hill farm. It was a really steep hill with a clump of trees at the very top.

This was our favourite place because it had lots of ridges and you were very lucky if you got to the bottom of this slope without being thrown off, but this all added to the fun of it. All the kids in the village would go and the adults too! I loved my walks along with my younger sister Jean and my little terrier dog Crackers.

Another favourite place was up Green Lane and over the railway bridge, then turning right next to the railway and up a little lane that ran alongside Jack Satts' fields.

We would take two sacks with us to collect wood from the hedgerows. When the farmer had laid a hedge we would gather all of the wood clippings for lighting the fire and larger pieces for putting on afterwards. Some of these could be quite big and so we would have to drag them all the way home.

The farmer often used to chase us, as I guess we must have made holes in his newly laid hedge, but he never caught us. On the other side of the road, through a wire fence alongside the railway, we found some lovely sweet red gooseberries. These small bushes were hanging with the lovely berries and they may have belonged to someone but no one ever came to pick them but us.

Mother loved wild flowers so we often took her a large bunch from Bluebell Lane. We would also take her a bunch of cowslips from the railway embankment. It must have been rather dangerous but we never saw the danger as kids. There was always plenty to do and never ever did we get bored.

Most nights after school and having had our tea, a gang of us boys and girls would meet on the square and enjoy games. Mostly running around, because no one kept still for very long. At weekends I enjoyed long walks with my dog and running errands for my mother and some of our neighbours.

We would often get tummy ache after stealing apples from the small orchards in the village, by having too many of them, but we all knew where the best trees and sweetest apples and plums were to be found. A really good tree was in the garden belonging to the vicarage. One evening there were three of us up this tree, filling our pockets and eating the deliciously sweet apples and dropping cores on the ground. Suddenly the vicarage door opened and the vicar appeared, looked around and came over to the tree and saw all the apple cores on the ground. He did not bother to look up or he would have caught us red handed, but we had a very lucky escape that time.

Down the croft from the square is Church Villas where two families of Bensons lived, next door to each other. Fisherman Jim and his wife had two sons, Walter and John, and two daughters whom I never met – they married and moved away from the area. Jim's brother Harold lived next door with his wife and son Thomas, a fisherman, and his sister Mary who was a lovely person and always seemed so busy.

In the orchard nearby was a stable for Jim's horse and a distance away was a pigeon hut. As well as being interested in football and known locally as a good player in the village team, his other interest was keeping racing pigeons. Many a time I would see him waiting patiently for the pigeons to return from a race, with his clock to record the times and probably hoping that he had won with these amazing birds.

From Church Villas you could take a short cut down a pathway through their market garden and past some greenhouses, which then brought you into the backyard of Septimus and Lizzie Benson, brother and sister of Jim. They lived together in their cottage in Main Street and neither ever married. Sep, as the villagers called him, was a really good fisherman with no fear at all. Looking back now I don't know whether this was a good or bad thing.

One day I arrived in the yard when Septimus was getting ready to go to the sands and he asked me if I would have a ride out with him to fish his nets not very far out from Humphrey Head. He was a really good friend of my parents and never missed calling in at our cottage if he was going to the Hope and Anchor public house for a pint. So, with knowing him, I said, "Yes, I would love to go." We arrived at the shore at Humphrey Head Holy Well dyke rather early on the tide and started to cross. Luckily for us both, Sep had a really good reliable horse and as soon as it dropped out of its depth and started to swim, it did not get excited. The cart was under the water and Sep lifted me onto the fore end, holding me with one arm and gradually pulling the horse round with the other hand. I will never forget the experience as the cold water came up to my waist and I found it hard to breathe as Sep gradually brought the horse slowly round and it swam for the shore. All this time, which seemed an age, I remember Sep saying to his horse – in true fisherman dialect – "Gu-lad, gu-lad, tha'll mek it." And it did!

Luckily for me on that particular day a Flookburgh man was gathering water from the Holy Well nearby. Sep lifted me out of the cart, dripping wet and feeling really cold and asked this man if he would kindly give me a lift back to Flookburgh, and he agreed to do so. I found out later that as the tide ebbed, his second attempt to cross Holy Well dyke was successful and he went on to fish his fluke nets. I got a good telling off from my parents and didn't go on the sands again without my father for a very long time.

The water from the Holy Well was taken to Heysham, then bottled and sold to the holidaymakers claiming that it would cure all ills. Miners used to come down by coach loads from Alston in Cumberland to take the water and almost every fisherman would take a bottle to the sands with them. Not anymore.

My late father, who was 101 years old when he died, was always interested in what I had been doing. One day I phoned him and said that I had taken a party out onto the sands and then on to the Holy Well to sample the water. Many had flasks and had filled them to take back home with them. "Oh hell mi lad, tha woint hear from then ivver a gen as it gives tha't runs!"

Nearly everyone noticed when some stranger appeared in the locality. Once a year an old tramp called 'flannel foot' passed through the village; he was harmless enough but us children all fled into our house and watched him through the window. He got his name because he always had his feet wrapped up in old rags. He came from Piggy Town and called in at the butcher's, almost opposite our cottage, where he was given some raw sausages, which he immediately ate. Some people gave him old clothes. Jane Dickenson, a neighbour of ours, gave him an overcoat and then he went on his way to Holker and probably spent the night in some building on Holker Mosses. A few years later this is where he was found dead.

Another person that came to the village was a knife sharpener. You could pay with a few old clothes and if you didn't want a knife sharpening, he would give you a plate and accept whatever you gave him.

Once a year we had a small fair come into a field at the bottom of the village, directly opposite the Crown public house. This field then belonged to Jim Benson, but now there is a row of houses and a nursing home called Bridge House.

On Saturday mornings it was always exciting when someone came along with a projector and set it up in the village hall showing old silent, black and white films. I remember some of them – Old Mother Riley, Abbot and Costello, and Laurel and Hardy. But the projector was forever breaking down and then all the kids would stamp their feet and whistle. We liked it when this happened because if the man could not fix it, then we all got our money back. I think we only paid a penny or two but it was fun.

Morecambe Bay viewed from White Creek, with the black lump of Humphrey Head in the far distance. (Peter Cherry)

The tide is out – and Humphrey Head glows orange in the late evening sun. (Paul Nickson)

WARTIME MEMORIES

At the outbreak of World War Two I was attending Flookburgh Junior School and everyone in the village was issued with gas masks. They came in strong brown cardboard boxes with a string attached, which enabled you to carry them over your shoulder. We had rehearsals in the school to see how quickly we could put them on in an emergency and also get used to them and we were told to carry them with us wherever we went.

One day a week, all of us from school marched with our teachers along Station Road to St John the Baptist Church, Flookburgh. We piled in through the door into the vestry and up the steps leading into the church, which was thought to be a much safer place for us youngsters than being in the school if there was to be an air raid.

By this time, my father had met and made friends with a Mr Briggs who came to live in Flookburgh with his wife and family. They had bought a house on Church Walk. Mr Briggs was involved with the army as a cook and told my father that there was to be an Army Camp and an aerodrome built at the bottom of Mile Road, on land belonging to East Plain farm.

Dad was eventually offered a job of putting up a large flag on the top of Humphrey Head which he did for a while. This involved climbing up the west face, which was quite dangerous. When this flag was flying, no-one was allowed to go either on the marshes or the sands as the army were practising shooting at large targets towed behind Avro-Anson aeroplanes.

There were ak-ak guns all along the sea embankments and at the camp. These targets were made of red silk; many a fisherman would find them out in the Bay and their wives made garments of them. Also shell cases were picked up by the fishermen, brought home and polished. Being brass they looked quite good and were used as ornaments and doorstops.

In the early stages of Cark Camp being built, dad would take me down onto the site. My memories are of seeing row upon row of tents being used by the soldiers and of roads being made from railway sleepers.

Almost every day, troops were landing at Cark station. We would watch them march across Flookburgh Square and down the mile long road with their tanks and target guns. It was quite frightening having all these soldiers about.

The sea recedes for many miles twice a day in Morecambe Bay and to prevent the enemy from landing on the sands, row upon row of concrete posts were put well down in concrete and stood up to about eight feet high. They had to withstand the tides so the lower areas of the Bay where changes occur frequently – and near to the river Kent and Leven – were left alone. But wherever you looked out over the sands from Flookburgh, Sandgate Shore, Humphrey Head, Cowpren

Point and across the Bay at Bolton-le-Sands and Hest Bank – all on higher ground – you saw row upon row in every direction.

The firm of Taylor Woodrow was contracted to erect these posts and they needed a large workforce. Quite a number of Flookburgh fishermen were employed in this task and some of them acted as guides to keep a watch out for the tides. Lots of Irish labourers also came over specially to be employed in this work. On many a day on high tides, there would have been very little time on the sands, whereas work would have been able to continue for most hours of the day on the low 'neap' tides.

When this work was completed my father received his call up papers to the war. This came as a shock to mum and us children, as dad had never been away from Flookburgh and spent most of his working life in and around the Bay, as had his father and grandfather before him. Although we were all terribly upset, I was the only male in the house and, although so young, was left in charge. I remember when it was time for dad to leave home and I sat at the top of the stairs and cried my eyes out uncontrollably.

On his first leave from the army he was taken ill and went to see his own doctor at Cark, Dr Charlton, who gave him a sick note to give to his commanding officer at Mansfield. He was then told to report to Conishead Priory at Ulverston, part of which had been taken over by the army as a hospital. It is now a Buddhist Centre. Dad was there for four weeks, until he was well enough to return to his battalion, and very soon after he left England by boat and we weren't to see him again for almost six years.

To help with the war effort, all metal gates and railings were cut off and taken away. You can see the stubs just showing in the stonework bordering houses and gardens in the village.

Whilst dad was away in the Eighth Army the row of cottages came up for sale, but mother not quite knowing what to do in his absence missed the chance of buying the one we occupied. They sold for £80 each. Today these same cottages are fetching a fortune. Mum was saving the money dad sent home for him to buy a horse and cart, plus nets and the like, to start fishing again. She also picked shrimps for Aunty Esther and dad's brother Uncle Jim, who always went by his nickname Carey. If it was dark when we arrived home, mum used to check out the house first to make sure there were no Germans hiding. Then we would lock the doors and draw the blackout curtains before we put the light on.

The Home Guard walked around the village at night-time to make sure no one had a chink of light showing. Our local bobby at that time was a terror and was known by the villagers as 'Blackout Joe'. Mum was a soft natured person and easily upset. The previous bobby was more laid back, but everyone's friend and he knew almost everyone in the village personally. Not now with this younger one, each and every household had to blackout the windows so that no flicker of light could be seen. Anyone found without proper blackout when he was on the prowl was in for it, as he was on to them like a ton of bricks. He frightened the life out of my mother one day when she saw him coming towards the front door of the cottage.

Unfortunately we were so poor that we couldn't afford to renew our dog licence, so before opening the front door to him she told me to take our terrier dog quickly out of the back door, thinking he would not know about it. Too late! He immediately said to mother that we had a dog with no licence and would have to pay a fine.

'Blackout Joe' was a heartless soul, because to pay the fine mother had to take in washing. As we had no electricity the water had to be heated on the open fire and the dolly tub and posser used. These hard times always remain in our memories, but we managed because we had such good neighbours who were kind and friendly.

To be at war was really frightening, especially at night when German bombers were heard droning overhead, heavily laden with bombs, en route for Barrow in Furness and the shipyard. To let people in the village know, a siren was sounded and families would take cover where they thought best for their safety. At first, mother put us children under the strong wooden kitchen table, but with dad being away from home, we were eventually offered a shelter a short distance from our cottage, down Moor Lane, belonging to Mr Avis and his son. This was a deep underground concrete basement, which always seemed so cold and uncomfortable. Mother used to take blankets for us, and to pass the time away, which to us children sometimes felt like forever, we used to sing old songs to keep us awake. When the all clear was given and the siren sounded, Johnny Wright was there to take us back to our own cottage safe and sound.

The only other family to use the shelter was Mrs Nicholls, her mother and all three children, Faith, Grace and brother Harold who was a baby. We never ever saw Jack Nicholls, the father, in the shelter.

Barrow in Furness is only a short distance away, as the crow flies, via Morecambe Bay and was heavily bombarded. Flookburgh got away very lightly, but a landmine was dropped into open fields on the west side of Humphrey Head and left a huge crater which almost everyone from the village at sometime or other went down to see for themselves. Hundreds of smaller incendiary bombs were dropped but most landed in the fields.

I remember watching a demonstration by the Fire Service showing the public how to tackle a blaze in an emergency, as the purpose of these smaller incendiary bombs was to set fire on impact. These demonstrations were given down the Mile Road, Moor Lane and on the roadway, opposite the fishermen's stables, including our own.

The village of Allithwaite did not get off so lightly. A huge bomb was dropped in Home Lane directly in front of one of the houses in a row, with severe damage to the property and others close by. A massive crater was found with burst water pipes spewing water everywhere. The house which caught most of the blast was almost cut in half. I remember this so well as a gang of us youths from Flookburgh heard about it and decided to walk to Allithwaite to see the damage done for ourselves. It was a frightening sight because you could see bedrooms with beds balancing over the edge in what was left of the upstairs floors. It reminded you of a child's dolls house, where you could open it up from the front and see both upstairs and downstairs with contents.

All other houses on Holme Lane suffered considerable damage with slates off roofs or windows blown out. The fields all around Allithwaite were littered with these smaller incendiary bombs, luckily so, for if they had been dropped in a built-up area they would have caused lots of problems.

A German aeroplane crash-landed in a field up Green Lane near to Appleby Hill and again, almost everyone from the village of Flookburgh trooped up to see this, but it was cordoned off by the Ministry and we were not allowed to touch it. It had nosedived into the side of the hill. An unexploded bomb was found in the orchard of Guides Farm, and for safety everyone in Cart Lane had to be evacuated from the area until it was made safe for them to return.

Grange over Sands had bombs dropped in Kents Bank Road, Fernleigh Road and behind the Co-operative, near to the late Ben Ward's shop. On the land opposite the ornamental gardens, high up and set well back from the main road, was property which belonged to the late Colonel Porritt and was left to the Parish Council of Grange over Sands. This caught a direct hit and was left like that for many years until it was decided to build a high-class residential home for the elderly with outstanding views out across Morecambe Bay. The building was called Yewbarrow Lodge.

At home, mum made us sit down and listen to the news on the radio to hear what was happening in the war, and we were not allowed to speak. I remember clearly the newsreader coming over on the radio and saying, "This is the news with Al-la-de-del- reading it." At least that is what the name sounded like to me. Dad was with the Eighth Army with Monty (Montgomery) and we, as a family, tried to follow whereabouts dad would be at that time.

We had the Daily Express delivered to our door every day by Joe Waller from Cark. His family had two small shops, one in Ravenstown near Flookburgh and the other in Cark, across from the Engine Inn. At Christmas time he opened up a showroom of children's toys which was exciting to see even if mother couldn't afford them.

To make a little bit extra money, mum made really beautiful rag dolls and elephants out of old clothes for Christmas presents. I used to sit alongside her cutting up rags to stuff. My fingers got so sore from using scissors. Cutting up these old clothes wasn't easy work, but we were warm and cosy and that was something.

Someone gave us some old vinyl records and we softened them in the fireside oven and shaped them into dishes and vases.

On a Sunday I always went to St John's Church of England, as I was persuaded to join the choir, and I don't think I missed once in all of the six years of dad being away from home in the army. The choirboys were paid sixpence a week old money, but never saw it. It was written down in a book and once a year we were taken on a coach trip to Blackpool and there the money was given us to spend. We were all boys as girls were not allowed to join the choir.

In Flookburgh we had three evacuees. One young girl came from Salford and stayed with Mr and Mrs Mayor in Main Street. Her name was Constance (Connie) Campbell; she was about my age and soon made friends with us all, boys and girls, and she attended Holker School.

School holidays and hot weather in the summer drew most families from Ravenstown and Flookburgh to the shore at Sandgate. Parents with prams and trolleys for younger children took a picnic and a kettle. They would ask Mr and Mrs Wilson at the nearby farm for hot water to make a brew for which they paid sixpence. On the shore a suitable place was found where everyone would lay out a blanket close to the edge of the small River Ea. Here the youngsters could play in the shallow water and their parents were able to keep an eye on them. Where the river turned sharp to run out into the Bay it was much deeper and all the older children would make for that area, which we all called 'the second beck'. This is where we would all swim and enjoy ourselves.

Both these areas were safe at low tide, but at high tide it was unsafe to be in the water without being a powerful swimmer. Sadly, Constance Campbell got into difficulties at high tide. Mr Mayor, who was with her at the time, tried desperately to save her but the strong current took him under and he was drowned. Connie was saved – but what a terrible tragedy to happen in such a way. This very sad news stunned everyone and made people more aware of the dangers.

My aunty Marie and aunty Muriel both had evacuees from London – respectively Anne Frost and Pat Howes. I remember them so well and they were quite wayward and hard to control. They attended Holker C of E school at the same time as me and had no respect for the teachers. The headmaster at the school was Mr Howitt and he was very strict. His nickname was Diggie Howitt, but no one would have dared to call him that to his face. I remember Pat Howes standing up in class and asking, "Sir, if a bean is a bean, what is a pea?" and the headmaster seemed very surprised, almost shocked, then replied. "I don't know." Pat quickly replied, "A relief, sir!" She was made to stand in the corner of the classroom for the rest of the lesson.

Another young girl came to live in the village and she was called Dora Edwards. Her mother had just died and her father was in the Navy. She came from Walney Island in Barrow in Furness to live with her granddad, Benny Wilson and her aunty in a bungalow behind Jack Nichols' garage.

Aunty thought she should dress in mourning. So when she mixed with all us youngsters she always wore long black stockings and a long black gabardine. She was a really nice person and soon made friends. The girls in the village persuaded her to change and wear ankle socks and a cardigan and so she started to look much happier and more one of us.

We village youngsters did enjoy ourselves. Food was scarce – on ration – but no one ever seemed to take any hurt. Nearly always on a Sunday teatime we had either prunes or custard, peaches with bread and butter or wobbly jelly and blancmange – and we loved it! Mother once managed to buy a flitch of bacon on the black market from a woman in the village who kept a couple of pigs in her old earth closet in the backyard. To hide it, we wheeled it home in my sister Jean's dolls pram, with dolls on top of it.

Lizzie Benson kept the pigs and she was a soft-natured person and treated them like pets. She even had names for her pigs and spent a lot of time with them, so you could imagine how she felt when the time came for one of her pigs to be slaughtered. I felt the same as I had been going down to Lizzie's pretty regular and she seemed to like me to go and see her.

The day of the slaughter saw lots of activity with all members of the family being involved. A stranger came along, probably the butcher and asked for the pig to be brought out into the yard. It squealed noisily before it was caught and humanely killed with a gun to its head. It was immediately lifted on to a wooden creel (a framework on legs) and no time was wasted as boiling water was poured all over it. Then the hairs were scraped off with a long, very sharp knife. The belly of the pig was then cut open and the blood caught in buckets and bowls and boiled to make Black Puddings. The pig was then cut up into various joints, rubbed with salt and left to hang and mature.

Animals were always at the forefront of my mind and at the village of Cark there was a riding and livery stables, owned by George Dickinson and run by his two sons Tony and Septimus – who went by the name of Robin. These stables were adjacent to the main road, halfway up Cark Hill and I passed it every day on my way to school. The late Arthur Cowperthwaite and Robert Dickinson were frequent visitors to the yard and suggested that I go along with them.

The love of horses drew me towards them as a child and still does to this day. I was therefore now in my element and went regularly before and after school to help feed and muck out the horses. Most of them were thoroughbred racehorses and, if we were lucky, we were repaid, not money-wise, but given the chance to ride out at weekends. We went over to Cartmel, through the park and seven acres, dropping down into Holker near Holker Hall and then back to the stables at Cark. Other than that, as young lads, we would ride the horses bareback and out to the fields.

I remember coming home from church on a Sunday evening in summer wearing my first suit with long trousers. Both my parents did not like the idea of me riding these thoroughbred horses, as they thought that I could get hurt or fall off. This did not deter me and from church that Sunday evening I went straight to the stables. There had been a ride out in the afternoon and the horses were stood in the loose boxes ready to take to the fields after they had cooled down. I was given a horse well known as a runaway, but I thought that it would stop when it got to the field gate. It did, but approached at full gallop and then stopped so suddenly that I went straight over its head into a muddy gateway. I was unharmed but my trousers were mucked up!

For what seemed an age, I didn't dare go home and when I did eventually pluck up the courage to return, my mother chased me round the backyard with a brush, caught me and then gave me a terrible hiding. She was still telling me off when we went in the back door. I caught my head on the door sneck and it would not stop bleeding. This really upset my mother as she was soft at heart and only thinking of my safety. She hugged me and we both cried and she said she was sorry for what she had done. This upset did not deter me from going to the stables the very next day.

School holidays were fun. If horses needed to be shod at the blacksmith's, one of us had to ride them there. One day, even though all my mates were very good riders, I got to ride the beautiful thoroughbred mare called Hym Buk. It was to be taken to Broughton smithy, and I said that I knew the way.

There was a blacksmith's shop at Flookburgh and one in Cartmel , which I had been to on several occasions, but I had never been to Broughton smithy so to get this job I had told a white lie.

I was riding bareback and given a leg up in the stableyard – and off we set. Beyond Cartmel we seemed to go such a long way without seeing Broughton or the smithy but I saw someone walking down the road and asked them if they knew the way. They replied, "Do you want Wood Broughton or Field Broughton?" This confused me so I turned the horse round and made my way back into Cartmel where I knew of a field that belonged to the Dickinsons. I opened the gate, took the head collar off the horse and he galloped into the sunset. I did not know that there was a stallion belonging to Mr Dickinson grazing in the next field. The stallion liked the look of the mare and jumped two lots of metal railings, then had the time of his life putting her in foal.

I was afraid to go back to the stables realising I would be in big trouble if I did, so I found another interest which was up Green Lane at the home of a retired judge, Judge Alsebrook.

He lived on a small farm with rambling gardens, swings, tennis courts, six Jersey cows and lots of large colourful Muscovy ducks which seemed to be everywhere. Judge Alsebrook had a land girl working for him and she took to me straight away. I used to follow her around and one day she harnessed up a small pony, put rubber shoes over the pony's hooves and yoked it up to a heavy roller to roll the lawns. I had never seen this done before but was so taken up with the little pony, which seemed so quiet and good to handle. I also noticed that in the barn was a beautiful trap and a set of harness and when I arrived at the farm one weekend I could not see anyone around. Judge Alsebroook was about the only person at that time with a motor car and it was not in the yard, so I thought that I would yoke up the pony into the trap on my own and go for a ride up to Cartmel and back. I just loved it, but as I drove this little pony and trap towards the farmyard gate I saw that the car was back in the yard and I would have some explaining to do. I did get a telling off for taking the pony out onto the roadway without permission, but I still visited when time permitted as there always seemed plenty to do that was interesting to me. I had other interests as well as horses and ponies!

In our village hall, there was a billiards and snooker room and on many an evening, especially dark winter ones, me and my pal, Roy Wilson would enjoy a game. The caretaker was a bit of a grump and his name was Peter Butler. Very strict with us lads, he was also the main bell ringer at Flookburgh's St John the Baptist church.

Collecting birds' eggs was also a hobby most young lads used to do. We would take one egg from each nest we found, prick two holes, one at either end, and then blow out the contents. The empty shells were usually kept in boxes with a little sawdust and they did look nice with all the different sizes and colours but rightly they are now protected and there is a fineable offence if you were to breach the law.

Sometimes a gang of us from Flookburgh would meet up with several of the Cark lads, Derek Thompson, Ken Bird, the late Bob Gilpin, Peter and David Newall, whose parents were the landlords of the Engine Inn. We would get together and walk down the road alongside the River Ea towards the shore and the railway crossing. In those days we didn't have much money in our pockets but we did something which we found exciting. When we heard a train approaching in the distance, we would all search our pockets for pennies and halfpennies, and if we were lucky someone would have a sixpence on them. We would lay them on the track and then we would hide down the embankment waiting for the train to run over them. After it had gone past we would find that our halfpennies now looked like pennies and the sixpences were made to look like shillings. We tried spending them at Joe Wallers little shop in Cark, but we were not very successful.

The things we got up to as lads – devilment but not malicious.

On a Sunday, a number of us would travel to Ulverston on the train and spend the whole of our time sitting in Tognarellas or Deganis's drinking warm Vimto and looking at the girls on nearby tables. That was it – we were all too shy to mix with strangers.

Now the war was almost at an end and our family was looking forward to seeing dad again after almost six long years away from home. One day I was walking to school with my mates and we saw this soldier coming from Cark in Cartmel railway station carrying this huge kit bag. It was my dad! My sister Jean was a little further down the road but came running as fast as her legs could carry her. There were lots of hugs and kisses and tears that day and needless to say we didn't go to school for the next couple of days.

FISHING FOR A LIVING

Eventually, dad had to start fishing again, for a living, in Morecambe Bay. So the money mum had saved whilst dad was away was now used to buy a horse and cart and fishing gear. We managed to buy a horse from a fisherman in the village with a lot of persuasion and it was a belter – very quiet and reliable. It was a dark bay mare, standing about 16.2 hands. Her name was Daisy. Then dad bought a set of second-hand harness from the saddlers at Greenodd.

We now needed a cart and Eddie Sands, a long-time fisherman friend of dad's who lived in Silverdale, said he had one that he would let us have. However, we would need to go and look at it to see if it was suitable. This was a sprung cart, ideal for shrimping, but we would also need a much heavier block cart for cockling. We eventually managed to gather together everything needed to follow the sands for a living.

We had stabling for the horse but no field at this time. Dad would yoke up our Daisy, take a scythe and sickle to sharpen the blade and go down the mile road to mow a cartload of grass from the road verges. A cartful would last a few days and, along with a good and regular feed of oats, would keep the horse pretty fit. In wintertime we had to buy hay from the Farmers' Supply, as the horse was kept inside.

Our stable was in the middle of a row of six, with Daisy in one and the store of hay for the winter in the next. There was an old horse in the adjoining stable and on the other side of ours were two horses belonging to a neighbour. All dad's gear, except the cart and his sea boots, were kept in the stable and along the back were newly tarred nets. In those days nets were not treated with preservatives as they are today, so we had to tar them before use and hang them up to dry.

Sadly, it was not long before disaster struck. We always went to bed in good time, ready to make an early start the next morning. One evening we were already in bed when we were alarmed at about ten thirty by shouting and a commotion outside. Looking out of the window we saw a fierce red glow in the night sky. We all threw on a few clothes and dashed outside.

The stables were built of wood and creosoted to help preserve them – and this helped the blaze! Horses were neighing and stamping in their stalls and people were screaming and shouting as horrible black smoke billowed up into the sky.

Dad tried to get near enough to look through the window of our stable but could see nothing of our Daisy. We thought she had gone down in the fire, and it was heartbreaking to think of him losing his horse. The old horse in the next stable was lying motionless on the floor and was a goner. The other two were still in their stalls and several people were trying desperately to free them by hacking away at the wood, which was on fire. They were using spades, axes, iron bars, anything they could find, whilst others were carrying buckets of water from the stream nearby in a vain effort to stem the fire.

The tarred nets and bales of hay fed the flames and it seemed impossible that any animal could still be alive. Then, one of the fishermen who owned one of the trapped horses broke into the burning stable and, although the smoke was densely thick, he managed to free the two animals.

Next, someone down at the watering spot shouted, "There's a horse over here!" It was our Daisy! She must have broken loose from the halter and smashed her way out of the back of the stables, but with the smoke being so thick, no one had seen her escape the fire. What a relief to all of us. Everything else had gone in the flames; cockle baskets, nets, stakes, oilskins and the winter food supplies – all lost. Mum and dad were in tears but when we found out Daisy was safe, at least we had something to start with again.

It was a miracle that any of the horses got out alive. The old one that died in the fire had been fastened in the stall with a chain and a strong leather halter and so had no chance of breaking free. The fisherman, Mr Cowperthwaite, who risked his life to save the two trapped animals, later received an award for his bravery, which everyone in the village thought he rightly deserved.

We never did find out how the fire started, though some people thought that a carelessly thrown cigarette end around newly tarred nets had caused the blaze - but we shall never know.

The following morning we went down to the stables to see the full extent of the damage. There was still lots of smoke and the horrible smell of burning. The charred remains of the old horse lay where he had gone down in the burnt-out stables. This was a terrible loss for us all, but we still had to earn a living from the sands and put all our efforts into getting the gear together once more, ready for work.

For many families in the Bay, including our own, cockle fishing was a main source of livelihood. Because of this, we were always on the lookout for new and more profitable grounds. For a number of years the cockles on the Flookburgh sands, though large and of very good quality, had been spread thinly over a large area. So, in 1946, dad and another fisherman, James Benson, decided to cross the sands to Silverdale and then on to Hest Bank having heard rumours of cockle beds over there. This was exciting for me, but I could only go cockling with dad at weekends and school holidays because I was still attending Holker C of E school.

Getting ready to go out cockling from the other side of the Bay needed a bit of organising. We had to take everything needed, and it would have to fit in the cart – jumbo, crambs, cockle baskets, riddle, a drag and a rake. We also needed something for the horse – a bale of hay and a bag of oats as it was wintertime. We also required sandwiches and flasks for ourselves. It was arranged that we met Jim Benson with his horse and cart in Flookburgh Square and then we were off on our journey. We made our way to Allithwaite, then up Jack Hill, of all places. I thought the horses would never make it up that very steep hill, which was about one in three, especially with their heavily laden carts. Eventually we did reach the top and then went along Allithwaite Road before turning down Carter Road, which was another steep hill. But this time we were going down. At the bottom of Carter Road we crossed the railway by the Cart Lane crossing and took the slipway onto the sands, which were very muddy, coming to the channel of the River Kent near to the shore.

We must have been a bit late on the tide as it had turned and was now running in, but the tides were neaps so dad and the other fishermen didn't seem worried

Flookburgh cocklers at work in the Bay. Although this photograph was taken over a century ago, the methods had changed little when I was a lad. A 'jumbo' (a wooden plank attached to a pair of handles) is being rocked to and fro to bring the cockles to the surface.

at all. The horses just made it through the channel, half swimming and now and then touching the bottom. Most of the tackle got a wetting but luckily the fodder for the horses had kept dry.

Now we had to set off for Silverdale at a good pace where arrangements had been made with a local fisherman, Eggy Hartley, to stable our horses overnight and where we would leave the next day to cross the sands to Hest Bank. It was a long walk from Eggy's to Silverdale station, to get the train home, where we knew mum would have a hot meal waiting for us to warm us up after being away for some time.

The following day we took the train from Cark station, near Flookburgh, back to Silverdale and walked to the farm. We fed and watered the horses. We then harnessed them up, yoked them in the carts and with everything loaded we were off on the turn on the tide. Out of the farmyard, down to the shore, across the marsh and then over the sands to the cockling grounds. Seemingly, this first day was only to look around, get our bearings and find the best places.

Although we found the cockles very good, dad and his mate Jim thought there would be better beds nearer to Hest Bank and Morecambe where true enough they were really rank or plentiful. There were already two local fishermen, who fished this stretch of sands for cockles, so we kept our distance.

For the next two years Hest Bank became almost a second home to us. We had stabling for the horses and could leave our carts and all our tackle there at the farm. This was up Hatlex Lane which was a short distance from the access to the sands at Hest Bank railway station.

We made some good friends among the porters and staff at the station and they let us use their cabin to eat our food in and also to sleep in when we had to be up and out on the sands very early mornings. However, I remember I didn't get much sleep as the line was so busy with express trains to Scotland and the north. They rushed alongside the old cabin, which seemed to shake with the vibration. I could only sleep in there with dad over the weekends and school holidays. After school on a Friday, mum would pack food for me to take on the train to Hest Bank station and this made it possible for me to stay over there and gather the cockles -when the tides were right.

We worked steadily on through the winter and spring and when summer came, music from Morecambe pier entertained us, so the days passed pleasantly enough. The cockle beds were really rank, plentiful and of good quality. It was only a short distance from where we were working to the shore, so we would load up one cart, usually Jim Benson's, as his horse, which he named Downy, was a flier. The cockles were taken to the station in no time to be unloaded, so that when we worked on until almost the last minute and found that the tide was chasing towards us, we then didn't have so much to load onto the carts.

The mill towns of Lancashire and Yorkshire were our biggest customers in those days. It is quite different today with most catches going overseas. After two years the cockles at Hest Bank had become rather scarce. As spring came some of the fishermen got unsettled and left for home grounds at Flookburgh to try for shrimps. Dad and I had a good order so decided that as long as we could find enough cockles to fulfil it, we would stick it out at least for the season and then we too could call it a day and come home.

CHAPTER TWO

Teenage Years

IN 1947 I LEFT SCHOOL at the age of fourteen and had to get accustomed to working with a horse and cart on my own. Dad had an eye for a good horse, so now we were looking for another and went over to Morecambe. We watched the horses at their work on the promenade, trotting back and forth from the Battery Hotel over to the beautifully lit Happy Mount Park. Many of these horses were brought over from Ireland to Heysham by boat and were then sold off to various buyers – mainly cabbie men. Fine weather brought in the holidaymakers during the summer and the rides along the promenade, especially when the Morecambe illuminations were at full swing were very popular and then the horses worked very hard. Dad got to know the cabbie men really well and would pick out a likely horse and then ask the owner if he would be selling at the end of the season. Sometimes they would rather sell than keep the horses through the winter – eating their heads off.

We sometimes had the opportunity of sitting up on the cab alongside the driver as the horse trotted merrily along the promenade. After a long day and then returning to the stables, dad would ask for a week's trial before buying the animal we had chosen. Most owners were agreeable to this - but not all.

Most of these horses took to the sands and water straight away, but you are always wary on the first trip into the Bay, the more so if it was in the season for trawling the rivers Kent and Leven for shrimps. If there was a breeze making the waters choppy, then this was something entirely different to what the horse had been doing his entire life and he could really play up. These times you needed assistance: one person to drive the horse forward at all times and someone to look after the net that was dragging behind the cart.

Shrimping was not only done in the daytime and about the end of August we often started working at night. When the tides were very low and the weather calm, conditions were ideal. Low tides meant that shrimps came into the shallow water and gathered near the side of the channel. If you could find a good place,

Shrimpers waiting for the ebb tide. My uncle Jim is on the cart, and on the extreme right is my dad's Clydesdale horse Charlie.

then the shallower the water the thicker and more plentiful would be the shrimps. We used to get out of the cart whilst the horse plodded on steadily with the net out, and you could see, by the light of the torch we always carried, the shrimps jumping over the beam and into the net. It really was a sight to see.

Each night there used to be a rush for the side of the channel where most of the shrimps would be found. No one wanted to be the inside cart at night working where the water was deep and the shrimps sparse. Sometimes it would be fairly level ground we were working on and our chances of a good catch were evened out. On the other hand – perhaps a mile or so along the channel – the banking would drop straight down and the water would be very deep, levelling off towards the other side. Then the outside cart would do well, even with its net half in the water and half in the sand, while the inside carts in the deep water found only very few shrimps and the rest of their catch would be crabs and suchlike. This was just the opposite of catches in the daytime when the shrimps were to be found in the deeper water and were usually much better quality.

There was a great deal to learn about shrimping with a horse and cart. With your horse going steady, you could judge what sort of catch you had by taking hold of the trawl rope and pulling the net towards you. When the time came for hauling it in, you would stop the horse, coil in the rope, lift the net on to the back of the cart and then ask the horse to move on and turn upstream. This ran the tail of the net right back and clear of the cart. Otherwise, the run of the water would have carried the tail-end of the net right under the cart and it would have got caught on the axle on the wheel nuts. Then we would have been in real trouble.

After a while, the horse got quite used to this turning, though when there was a row of horses and carts more or less in line with one another you needed to have an obedient animal. When the first horse started to turn upstream and with quite a flow of water still on the ebb, the next man had to get his net on to the back of the cart in quick time. Otherwise it was almost impossible to pull the net onto the cart, so we had to turn quickly downstream and try again.

We always had a spare coil of rope in the cart in case the horse dropped out of his depth in the channel where we were shrimping. We could then let out some rope to take the weight of the net off him and let him swim along more easily until his feet touched the bottom again. Then we would stop and pull in the spare rope, hoping that this didn't happen again as such unforeseen things could be very frightening. These were the times when our lives depended on having a really steady and reliable horse.

I was lucky. My first horse took to the water straight away and you would have thought that it had been on the sands before. He was a dark bay gelding, standing at 16 hands, strong boned, but with very little feather. There was always excitement in the village among the fishing families whenever a new horse was joining the fleet. I couldn't wait for the day for this horse to arrive by train in the siding at Cark & Cartmel station.

Dad would have known in advance the arrival time of the passenger train into Cark and we were there in good time. As the train pulled into the station we could see that the last carriage was the railway horsebox. After the passengers had got off and all was clear, the porter blew his whistle and the train started to shunt backwards into the siding.

The porter was carrying a long wooden pole with a metal hook on the end. As soon as the train stopped at the buffers, he quickly ducked down onto the line between the passenger coaches and the horsebox and prized apart the coupling, releasing it with the help of this long pole. Once this was completed the train was free to move away and continue on the rest of its journey. Now we could drop down the side ramps and lead our new horse back through the village and into the stable.

He had travelled well and not sweated up. That was a good sign and he almost kept us running as dad led him on a rope halter – to new beginnings. We decided to call him Banner.

This was now the end of the summer season and shrimps were getting scarce with the colder weather, so we started cockling as we had some very good orders. Banner took to the sands well and dad and I were really pleased with him. Dad didn't have any grazing so he was stabled throughout the winter and fed on hay and oats. When spring came along I started shrimping with him out in the Bay, alongside my father and other Flookburgh fishermen. He did everything I asked of him.

OUT ON THE SANDS

One night dad and I, along with several other Flookburgh fishermen, left the village for the shrimping grounds. There were about fifteen fishermen all with their horses and carts. It was a still, calm night with no moon and no wind at all. We all travelled down the mile-long road over the marsh, or cockle road as it was at one time called, and out into the Bay.

For a young lad, this was a kind of excitement for me but still a little bit eerie. Each cart would follow close behind the one in front, but it was so dark you could hardly see even your own horse. Looking back now at what those sand horses did for their owners to make a living, they were worth their weight in gold. As we arrived at the shrimping grounds, we made our nets ready to drop from the back of the cart. Then the horses made their way into the water, the splashes from their hoofs lighting up just like sparklers. Banner, being new to the job, had never seen 'foxfire' –as we called this phosphorescent glow – and he was petrified.

Every movement of the horses' hooves in the water sent up a shower of sparkling drops into the dark night. As the cart in front of me moved out, its wheels threw up a cascade of shining water right in my horse's path and frightened him so much that I could not control him. He just wanted to get anywhere out of the foxfire and this for me was really frightening. Dad decided to take Banner and I took Daisy, who was a quiet, experienced animal.

The foxfire had to be seen to be believed. Even when you had hauled in your net and emptied your catch of shrimps into a box, and were running your fingers through them to sort out the seaweed, you didn't need a torch because they were all aglow.

These sparks flickered around the spokes of the wheels, the hubs and the nets. We could see the whole shape of the nets glowing with phosphorescence. If only this could have been photographed, but you could never tell when it would occur. I have seen it very few times in my life in spite of all my time on the sands. Shrimping with a horse and cart, and thus activating the water, showed to the full the true brilliance of the foxfire.

There was a lot to learn as a youngster following the sands for a living, but luckily I fished with my father and he taught me a lot. For example, there was no obvious pleasure going out into the middle of Morecambe Bay in thick fog, but we still went and found our way safely there and back again. To one who follows the sands everything has a meaning. In particular, you have to keep a sharp eye open all the time for changes in the way the dykes and gullies have been left by the tide. You are not going over the same area every day, since the sands change with every tide, which fills the Bay twice every twenty-four hours.

People may wonder why we never used a compass. We were never brought up to use one. We were taught to read the sands.

There are so many dangers out there to target the unwary. In my younger days of fishing from a horse and cart, I have seen two horses go down in quicksand whilst trawling the River Leven for shrimps. Although the shafts were hacked away and the horses were freed from the carts, they were well and truly stuck in the sands. When the tide was on the turn the fishermen had to leave the channel and all they could do was stand and watch as the tide lapped over the horses and eventually covered them. What seemed like an age was perhaps only a few minutes and, with the buoyancy of the animals and the struggling, they popped up to the surface and swam to the side to the awaiting fishermen and other horses. Quite a remarkable experience and almost a miracle!

I had a really frightening experience with a horse which I bought from a farmer at Leece, near Ulverston. He was a really good-looking dapple grey and a good mover but steady in the water when pulling the cart and trawling for shrimps. I hadn't had him many weeks when we reached the shrimping grounds just as the moon was coming up. It was a lovely summer's night – perfect for shrimps. There were only three of us fishermen out that night and the horses splashed into the water, which was about a foot deep as we dropped our nets from the backs of the carts. I was in the middle, with the other two being one either side of me. Suddenly there was a drop of three feet or so and my horse fell. I naturally thought he had stumbled, but he lay there and didn't even struggle.

I jumped from the cart at once, grabbed his head and held it above the water. The other two fishermen, seeing what had happened, couldn't get their nets onto their carts quickly enough and drove to the side where one man stayed with their horses while the other waded in to help me.

I knew by now that my horse had not just stumbled. His nostrils were wide, his eyes staring and his breathing heavy and irregular. Going down as he had, the harness had tightened, so nothing could be loosened. Luckily I always carried a knife, so I cut the top strap from the harness, and also the leather backband and breaching straps.

Now he was free of the cart. We thought he would get up but he didn't. We used all of our strength and energy in pulling and eventually had to use force! He then came up unsteadily on to his legs and we led him to the side. We feared of him dropping down again so one of the fishermen kept him moving around whilst two of us went back into the water to retrieve the cart. We found that because of his weight on the shafts as he lay in the water, they had been partly submerged in the sand, so the only way to get the cart out was to go in with one of the other horses and tow it out. This worked, and towards the side we came. Because the harness had been cut, we decided to tow my cart behind one of the others, while I led my horse slowly home.

I bedded him down in his stable and rang the vet. He was a very good man and came at once. After a thorough examination, he told me the horse had suffered a severe heart attack. He gave him an injection and said we would see how he was in the morning, but he didn't give much hope. Early the next morning as I opened the stable door, I could see the horse lying dead. It was a great blow as I had just got attached to him and he was so steady and reliable at the job.

My dad said at the time that as sad as it was to lose the horse, had this happened in daylight hours when we trawled deep channels, I might not have been quite so lucky. At least we did make it back to the stable. Now we had to look for another horse.

MARKET DAYS

My mother became friendly with Annie Reagan, as Annie and her mother were very experienced at picking shrimps (taking the husk from the shrimp). They would sit at a table for long hours, shelling shrimps and they were probably two of our best pickers. This helped us, as the more shrimps you could get picked the more money we would make. There were now two of us with horses and carts regularly going out in the Bay to the shrimping grounds.

Annie and Mary Reagan lived in Main Street, in one of a row of small cottages which all had allotments at the rear of their properties. Annie mentioned to my mother that her father was thinking of retirement. He was going to sell his land and take life a little easier. The land was roughly an acre, well set up in small plots of different vegetables with a sixty-foot greenhouse and about thirty feet of cold frames full of cucumbers.

Dad was really interested and wasted no time in going along to see Mr. Reagan. I was now fifteen – going on sixteen – years old and a good help to my parents and so the deal was done. Mr Reagan put his trust in dad and allowed him to pay cash in two instalments. I knew little about gardening but was willing to learn. With the garden came a flat cart called a barrow and the right to stand on Barrow in Furness outdoor market on Wednesdays and Saturdays. Mum and dad would take the early train with the flat cart loaded up with vegetables, along with shrimps, cockles and flukes which we had caught ourselves.

On market days I used to go to the sands, sometimes according to the tides. I would be out there very early before dawn, fish the fluke nets and get back home with the catch of lovely big fresh fish for my parents to take with them to the market. If I wasn't going to the sands, my sister Jean and I used to go down the mile road and onto the marsh very early in the mornings to collect mushrooms. You had to get there early before anyone else, sometimes setting off from home at 5am to arrive there just as it was coming daylight. We also collected wild blackberries out of the hedgerows near to the marsh. The bushes caught the morning sun so in this area the blackberries were always early and good quality. We also picked watercress out of the streams.

As there were no supermarkets in those days the people of Barrow loved this food and we did a roaring trade. My parents just loved going to the market and, although I did go there with them now and again, I never really took to it and preferred going to the sands.

Horse-drawn transport was still very popular and, whilst helping out on the market one day, I couldn't help taking notice of a really grand type of horse yoked to a milk lorry on rubbers, with the driver delivering milk around the town. Never in a million years did it cross my mind that one day we would own it.

When I was fifteen we moved to the creeper-covered house in Main Street, Flookburgh, shown on the right of this photograph. This view dates from the era before the motorcar was commonplace.

The allotment at the rear of the Main Street house enabled us to take up market
gardening. Hard at work planting lettuces in this 1956 photograph are (left to right)
Frank Lomas, my dad and me.

It was not very long before dad spotted an advert in our local weekend paper. Barrow in Furness City Council was making a changeover from horse-drawn vehicles to the more modern motor transport. All the horses were now redundant and were advertised for sale by tender.

I knew of one or two of the Flookburgh fishermen as well as my father who put bids in for these horses but unfortunately they were all sold to a farmer at Marton near Dalton in Furness. The farmer then sold them individually at a profit. I remember travelling over to the Barrow in Furness Council stables, where we were shown all the horses, their vehicles and their tack. The majority were quite heavy and not suitable for the sands but ideal for work on a farm. We were then shown this strapping strawberry roan horse, which stood all of seventeen hands, and straightaway said this was the one that would interest us. About a week later, when dad and I travelled over to Marton to the farm, the big strawberry roan was grazing in a nearby field and we were told that he was still for sale, so we bought him.

In no time I had him out on the sands below Aldingham, wading in the tide. Albert Edmondson, a young fisherman from that side of the Bay, offered to go with me. It is always best policy to have two people in the cart when trying out a horse new to the sands, but surprisingly this big strawberry roan took to the water as if it had been doing the job all of its life. It was good flat sand there and a safe area but I was really pleased with the way he performed.

SHRIMPING IN THE BAY

Around this time a few of the Flookburgh fishermen had found grazing for their horses and were following this side of the Bay trawling for shrimps. These were of good quality and much bigger than the shrimps being caught at Flookburgh. Dad managed to rent a field up Leece Lane not very far from the shore and, after getting the horse shod at Leece, I shrimped with him over that side of the Bay in the Mussel Hollow – a very deep area of water. I had got to know Albert Edmondson and his father Wilf quite well by now. Wilf worked for the council but at weekends he would be out in the Bay shrimping throughout the season. They lived on the coast road, a stone's throw from the sands. They also set nets to catch the plaice.

As the shrimp season drew to an end I brought my horse and cart back across the sands to Flookburgh. Dad and I were to start cockling through the winter, but this was nothing for a big leggy horse like him. Spring came along – a cold one – and in March the water was still very cool. The horse just didn't like being in the water at all and was almost unmanageable. It was a fairly wild day, blowing and blustery with white surfs coming up against him. He suddenly reared and this was scary, as we were in deep water. All the other fishermen moved away and, as each wave hit him, up and down he went.

I eventually managed to get him to the side and one of the fishermen shouted, "Put a bag over its ee-ad." (In dialect 'ee-ad' means head.) I hadn't a bag, so I took off my jacket and fastened that over his head. Then I tried getting him back into the much shallower water – but he wasn't having it. He just kept going backwards onto the shrimp net. I eventually gave up after that and took him home. Being such a big horse and in deep water when he reared, the cart was right up and I had a job of holding on.

I was now thinking of my dad's words . "If they have a bit of blood in 'em, keep off 'em. They're no good to us – too fiery!" A cross-bred horse, one with a bit of feathering about it, was better for our work. I didn't really want to take any more risks whilst out in the Bay shrimping with this horse, so dad and I travelled over to Morecambe and did a trade-in. He was now back on dry land pulling a Landau on Morecambe front, giving enjoyment to the holiday makers.

We replaced him with a horse which had been brought over from Ireland just one week previous. Dad and I were able to ride on the cab with the driver and this took us on a journey to Snatchems, alongside the River Lune. High tides cover the road but this was well marked out with wooden posts either side showing the depth of water. This horse was a really good mover and very strong boned and when the water was almost knee-deep it never seemed to bother him at all.

We arrived back at the stables at Poulton Square after dropping off the passengers on the promenade and dad had to pay money to the owner dealer Arthur Turner. This was a much younger horse and I can honestly say it turned out to be the best one I ever had on the sands of Morecambe Bay. With being broken to an open bridle over in Ireland, dad and I yoked her into a single farrow plough in the market garden and she was as steady as a rock. She went along as straight as a dye, and once in the cart she was a really good mover and could almost catch pigeons at the trot.

Life for me seemed to be bed and work and more work! Finding a market for the shrimps was sometimes very difficult and though for a while we had good orders from one of the northern coastal towns, we found later that we had a job to get the money in. It was far too costly to have to make the journeys to the other side of the Bay just to chase the bad payers. My sister and I therefore decided to take a basket, lined with white cloth, full of really big picked shrimps we were getting at the time, and hawk them round Carnforth. We would set off, each with our own basket covered with a white muslin cloth, and we would go on the train.

We both enjoyed going round the houses and meeting different people. They were really good customers and once they knew the days we would be going, they would leave a dish with their order and the money on the window sill. Carnforth was a very good fish town for us in those days. It seemed that as one market closed another one opened up. We felt that luck was with us.

Then came a setback. Dad became ill so I had to take the horse and cart and go to the cockling grounds. My sister Jean came along with me and the other fishermen were very good and kept an eye on us while dad was unable to work.

We did fairly well, as we were both very close and got on well together. Mum managed to boil the cockles with our help, though we missed dad terribly and had to keep asking him how to do this, that and the other. But this is the way to learn and I could soon do the job quite well – young as I was.

Meanwhile we had found a spot where shrimps were plentiful. But marketing them was becoming a problem, until dad hit on the idea of salting them down in wooden barrels until such a time as we could find a market. Salted hard, they could be kept indefinitely and we could hold on to them until we could make money on them.

Such a time was just around the corner. In 1949, late one evening, a knock came on our door. On answering it we found a good-looking chap in his early fifties. He said he had been sent from London and would be interested in buying shrimps. He told us of the premises he had in mind and said that until the firm got properly organised he would collect all our shrimps from the door. This he did regularly – on an old butcher's bicycle! He carried the shrimps in a box on the front in the same way that the butcher's boy of old used to bring the meat round to the door. The catches he collected from us were sent down to London – no doubt for the thriving markets there, where the hotels were beginning to use the lowly shrimp in some quantity. Later the collection of the shrimps was done in an old London taxi, which was a step up from the bicycle.

This was going to be a good thing for the village fishermen, and we ourselves were able to sell from the barrels the surplus shrimps we had stored. We were lucky to be the first to be called on by this man, as it was early days and he could only take shrimps from one or two fishermen. Shrimping was to become our main job now that we had secured our orders, sold our surplus and had a market on our doorstep. There was no limit to what we could catch; we were limited only by the amount we could get picked.

For the picking or shelling of the shrimps we were fortunate in having some very good workers. Before the husk could be separated from the fish, the shrimps had to be properly boiled; this made all the difference to the work of the pickers and dad was an expert at the boiling process.

When shrimps are first caught they are a greyish colour, and almost transparent. They are emptied from the nets into boxes and the crabs, small flukes and jellyfish are thrown back into the water. When the fisherman reaches home the shrimps are put in a boiler, the old cast iron type of washing boiler is still widely used in Flookburgh. The water must be right on the boil before putting them in, and then they are given a good stir round.

This makes sure that they are all evenly boiled. From the time of putting them in the boiler it takes about ten to fifteen minutes for the first boiling. Less time is needed for the second and third boilings as the water keeps its heat.

In years gone by, when the shrimps were taken out of the boiler they were spread on hessian sacks to drain and dry. Then they would be riddled and the small ones taken back to the sands where the seagulls would be waiting for them. Today, shrimps have to be riddled out on the sands alive, instead of bringing back the whole catch; the law requires that the small ones be put back into the water to grow. Nor are hessian sacks used any longer. It is impossible to get them now that they have been widely replaced by plastic and today the shrimps are drained and dried in trays.

As well as our regular pickers we were able to get some extra helpers who were really good. These were mainly Polish and Italian families who were housed nearby in what during the war had been an RAF training camp, These families were shown how to shell the shrimps and after a week or so they got the hang of it. They were doing us a real favour and also making themselves some extra cash. For several years these people were allowed to stay in their huts – nissen huts they were called – and I suppose they were really glad to have them after what they had been through during the war. They kept their homes spotlessly clean and with their little gardens surrounding them they looked very cosy. We found these families easy to get on with and quietly spoken. Some of them moved away to the towns where they could find better paid work than was available in this area, but a few stayed on to settle into village life and are still here to this day.

A TASTE OF FREEDOM

Fishing the Bay was hard work and unearthly hours but a healthy life and from leaving school this was all I wanted to do – just be a fisherman the same as my father and grandfather. But I was now at the age where I needed a little bit of freedom at weekends and also a few hobbies. My good friend Bryan Shaw and I shrimped and cockled together out in the Bay and so quite often on high tides at weekends we would go shooting - mainly ducks and oystercatchers - down on the shore at Cowpren Point. Brian was a good shot. I was not used to having a gun as my parents were dead against this at first, but they eventually gave into me and allowed me to buy a double barrel twelve-bore shotgun.

The birds would fly up close to the shore at high water and we had an excellent hideout behind a wall. In those days the sea birds were not protected as they are now and we got lots of oystercatchers and ducks. Rabbits were numerous on the farmland at Canon Winder farm, near Cowpren Point, and Frank Philipson was good and allowed us to go on his land because of the destruction they would cause in the green crops. Brian had a couple of ferrets which we used and we got many rabbits.

One day I was out shooting on my own in a big field close to the shore. I was pleased with myself as I had bagged three large rabbits and was on my way back across the field when all of a sudden I heard the sound of a hunting horn and could not believe what was happening. I ran like the wind and cleared the short wall which led me onto the shore. Dare I look back, just a peep? I was so scared because all I could see was horses and riders and a pack of hounds coming towards where I was hiding. It went through my mind how hounds have sometimes savaged a fox and I had this horrible feeling of fright. I had visions of me and my rabbits being torn to pieces. I kept terribly still until all went quiet.

The hunt had turned away from me into another field and was I glad. I set off for the shore at Sandgate as fast as my legs would carry me and when I arrived home I skinned and gutted the rabbits and then mother made a huge rabbit pie, which in those days we had quite often and all the family did enjoy. I never told my parents of the frightening experience, but I did keep away from that area for a while.

My father was a strong person in mind and body and we both worked hard on the sands and in the market garden. He used to say to me that hard work never killed anyone "mi lad", although he did encourage me to join our local Flookburgh Silver Band – attending a practice once a week. We practised in the band room which was upstairs above the bar in the Hope and Anchor public house. A few young lads including myself would arrive earlier than the main practice to be taught by Sep Benson who was the conductor at the time.

He would hang a cornet on a length of string from the ceiling of the bandroom and encourage us to blow into the instrument without puffing out our cheeks. When we did eventually master that side of it and began reading music, Sep would get us together, then with his foot, prominently and loudly, he would stamp out the beat – one, two, three or four beats. The publican below and his customers were not happy with this noise going on above their heads. Eventually the band lost the use of the band room and then had to look for somewhere else to have their practices. They were lucky, because the snooker room in the village hall came empty. Popularity of the game had fallen with very few villagers attending any more so the snooker and billiard tables were carefully taken down and stored in a room downstairs. This was to become the band room and so every band member was well pleased.

Some of the bandsmen were fishermen and fishermen's sons but all the band members were from the village of Flookburgh. Through the winter months these band practices were always well attended and when spring and summer arrived it was a nice change to play outside at various engagements. There were many: Barrow Carnival at Barrow Park; Ulverston Carnival; our own Flookburgh Carnival which ended up on the square with the band playing for most of the afternoon; Warton village Carnival near Carnforth; and Grange Carnival.

We also had a day out at Morecambe with the band when we played in the grounds of the swimming baths where the judging of the beauty contest was being held. Afterwards us younger band members had a great time on the funfair for a while. We were on the dodgem cars when I was rammed from behind and my hat accidentally flew off onto the floor. Sparks immediately came from it as the bandsmen's hats had a metal strip bound around the peak. I was unable to retrieve my hat till the end of the ride because of the surface being live. It was badly burned, but I was not unduly worried as I only wore it when asked to do so. From then on no one seemed to mind.

There were music festivals at Millom and Morecambe in which a few of the band members took part and did well. As I mentioned earlier, when I joined the band I at first played the cornet. As time passed and I gained more experience, I changed over to the tenor trombone, sitting alongside an experienced player and learning all the time. The late Charlie Rowlandson was the tenor trombone player and soloist and when he left the band I was given the place of first trombone. In a full band there would be four trombones, first, second and third tenors and one bass, but for a while I was the only tenor with the late Bill Bland playing bass. Later came Mike Garnett and Derek Dawson but all three of us young players had a lot to learn.

As the band did not have a resident conductor, either Sep Benson or Harold Manning – both of them fishermen – would take up the baton, but that meant we were a player short each time. Eventually an experienced conductor from the Barrow in Furness Steelworks Band attended the practices each week, travelling by train, and he really brought the band on.

A year or so later the band was taken over by Herbert Sutcliffe – the musical director and conductor of Barrow in Furness Shipyard Works Band. He was great and everyone respected him. When he eventually got to know the band, he realised where extra instruments would make all the difference and would bring along players from the Shipyard Band to the practices. At first we were short in the trombone section and he brought with him two excellent players – first and

Flookburgh Carnival ended up on the square with the band playing most of the afternoon. Here I am in 1956.

second trombone, Jimmy Everett and Roy Dancer. I now sat in third position and felt very nervous as these two were really experienced players and I was so young.

I was told by Mr Sutcliffe that I had a lovely tone on the trombone and must stick at it with lots of practice. He asked if I would mind travelling over to Barrow in Furness to his home where he would willingly teach me as he thought that I would make a promising player. I jumped at the idea, took his advice and felt really privileged. Other young members were helped in the same way.

As the band improved, there came a time when Mr Sutcliffe thought it was good enough to take part in contests. I remember playing at Darlington, Belle Vue, Manchester and Blackpool Tower Ballroom, but almost everyone suffered nerves once we were on the stage to play to an adjudicator and an audience. We were told that we could buy something at our local chemist, supposed to be good for settling nerves. This did not make a scrap of difference, but I suppose to take part in these contests was quite an ordeal for our band from a small village. However, as time went on, every band member was really made up when we eventually qualified in the 1950s for the finals in Kensington Town Hall in London.

WORK AND PLAY

I have always enjoyed going out into the Bay from a very early age and have encountered all kinds of weather. Changes can come suddenly, and you have to be prepared for all of them. Thunderstorms, with the rain lashing down, and strong gale force winds too. But fog is the worst hazard and I was lucky in having the experience of my father to call on. He also taught me never to go through large areas of shallow water. This can be as dangerous as putting your head in a noose, especially in fog.

When you go out there, you want to be able to come back, so you must keep to the drier areas and take notice of everything as you go along. To one who follows the sands, everything has a meaning. In particular you have to keep a sharp eye open all the time for any changes in the way the tide has left the sand and the dykes. The smaller drains or dykes don't change quite so much to one who has been brought up to notice every little difference as I was. The sand horses truly amazed me on how good they were to work with in the dark. A horse new to the sands would take a little time to get used to following wheel marks made on the outward journey, but an experienced animal was able to follow them even in the dark. You could even sit in the front of the cart with your back to the horse and he would bring you home.

There was quite an industry of shrimp fishermen in the village. When they all arrived home with their catches, the fishermen's wives or some member of the family would have already lit the boiler, with the water on the boil and ready to put in the shrimps.

The womenfolk in the village would never attempt to hang out their washing when the shrimp carts were arriving home, as almost everywhere you looked you would see black smoke billowing from the chimneys in the boiler houses. As already related, the shrimps had to be boiled and then spread outside to drain and dry in hessian sacks. The smell of the steam and the aroma from the freshly boiled shrimps was really something and at that time Flookburgh was certainly a fishing village.

You never saw a poor horse belonging to a fisherman. They worked hard, but were always well fed and looked after. They had to be, because our livelihoods depended on them. After stabling the horse and giving him a feed, then letting him cool down for a while, it was time to take him out to the field to graze. Dad had a rough area of land at the bottom of the mile road on the Cark Airfield, which belonged to the Ministry. I always rode my bicycle with the horse in a halter trotting alongside, as I took him out to the field.

Our lives revolved around work and more work, as I was often on the sands and between the tides working on the market garden. Dad fished the Bay apart from the two days a week following Barrow Market, so we were always busy. All work and no play – I was told that it was no good for me.

My pals, Bryan Shaw and Jack Manning, both had motorcycles. I pestered my parents, but one or two young lads from Flookburgh had lost their lives in the past. Although there were very few cars on the roads, these accidents had put my parents against me having my own motorcycle. No matter how careful you were, accidents would still happen. Eventually they gave in to me and I became the owner of a brand new Douglas 350cc, light blue in colour, bought from Harry Holmes in Dalton in Furness.

At weekends I was now able to go out with my mates, mostly to Ulverston. Each Saturday night was dance night at the Coronation Hall. On Friday nights we went to most of the hunt balls, which were held at Broughton in Furness, Grizebeck, Greenodd, Bowness and Silverdale during the winter months. There were much smaller gatherings held in the village halls or institutes and we never seemed to get to know anyone at these events.

Ulverston was our regular place and usually the Sun Inn opposite the Market Hall was our first port of call. After a few visits we met up with other lads with motorcycles and made friends.

The 'Corro' as it was called had a very good resident band and so it did get a really good following. I enjoyed dancing and met many nice young girls. As I was with my mates, we all three of us fancied the same ones but they were always taken. When it came to the last waltz, these nice young girls would dance with their boyfriends and we would be standing there looking very disappointed. But we always had a really good time and enjoyed ourselves.

To make a change, a few of us from the village would fancy a day out at Morecambe, so we would take the train from Cark station changing at Lancaster, then on to Morecambe station near the promenade. First stop, the fairground and then a good look at all the horses trotting up and down on the prom, eyeing them up as suitable for following the sands.

Morecambe was always enjoyable in those days. It just seemed to have everything, especially when the illuminations were taking place. Two

The blue Douglas motorcycle that became my pride and joy. My sister Jean is on the front.

fairgrounds, three jolly good dance halls, the Winter Gardens, the Floral Hall and the Pier – and the best chippies to be found anywhere. There was also an excellent restaurant at the West End of Morecambe, opposite the Battery up one of the side streets, which was called the Galleon. We young lads often went there to get a really good meal before catching the last train home.

I have happy memories of a venue back along the promenade near the Winter Gardens. Adjacent to the Dance Hall, down several steps into a basement, was a saloon with lots of tables, a very busy bar and a resident dance band. On the door we always met this person dressed in uniform and looking very smart. He was built like an oak tree – very strong and stood about 6ft 6in tall. We lads couldn't ever see anyone wanting to argue with him. With visiting quite regularly at weekends, we got to know him and he also found out a little bit about us. He knew that I played the trombone and invited me to take my instrument along and join in with their band, which I did on more than one occasion. This was mainly busking, not playing from music, but I had got quite used to that and thoroughly enjoyed myself. I always kept up my practices and playing at home and my father would always encourage me to play old tunes and songs for him. He just loved to sit and listen to me.

After the summer season of band engagements came to an end, our Flookburgh Band always played at the village Cenotaph on the morning of Remembrance Sunday. In the afternoon, joined by family members and band enthusiasts, we travelled by coach to Grange over Sands. We then marched for the British Legion with their members, through the town and down Main Street to the Cenotaph in the grounds of the ornamental gardens. After several hymns were sung, Sid Bland played 'The Last Post' which was always very moving. Afterwards, at the Crown Hotel at the top of Main Street, a very nice tea was always given to the band members who thoroughly enjoyed the occasion. It finished with lots of fancy cakes.

Although I always looked forward to playing with the band at their engagements, following the sands was my choice when I left school. Most of my school pals went into a trade. Fishing was not classed a trade, but I had made up my mind. I wanted to follow in the footsteps of my father and grandfather and I also was told that grandmother was a really good cockler.

Cockling is in season the whole of the year, but wintertime is the busiest with all fishing families working the cockle beds. Shrimping was another important source of our income and this was done with a net trawled from the back of the cart, so our horses needed to be able to move quickly at both the walk and the trot. The carts they had to pull were on tall wheels, so that we could go in fairly deep water without the shrimps floating about in the cart bottom. The horse needed to respond quickly if you were working at the inside position with at least fifteen fishermen with their horses almost in line gradually pushing you into deeper waters. It needed a very good horse to be able to excel itself to get out of trouble, or it would have had to swim for it. My father had owned some really good horses in his time, but he was one for a change when he was much younger. He told me that his mother had said he changed his horses more often than he changed his socks, but I never knew whether this was true or not.

A FASTER HORSE

I only knew that I was now coming up to eighteen years old and I wanted a horse that could get a move on. I did own a really reliable horse, black with white blaze and two white socks. It was a picture to behold – and very reliable in the water. But if I was unlucky enough to have got the inside position and in the river where there was a fast flow, then there was a real problem. When I asked the horse to get a move on, he just lifted his head each time so I walloped his rump with the reins. This was no good as the net behind the cart was catching us up and in danger of getting fouled on the wheel nuts.

I told dad that I needed a much faster horse for shrimping, so he suggested that I travel round the other side of the Bay to meet up with a fisherman friend of his who had about six horses on contract, carting sea-washed turf from the shore at Silverdale. We had no telephone in those days but you got to know other fishermen out in the Bay. There were two of them at Silverdale, Bill Hartley and Eddie Sands. I remember travelling round on my motorcycle and going out shrimping with Eddie Sands and his grey gelding 'By Gum'. It certainly was a mover. When we arrived at the shrimping grounds, Eddie dropped the net from the back of the cart and it seemed alright, maybe a little bit fast at first but I thought it would settle itself down once we got into deeper water. Eddie didn't have any fear at all and in no time we were trawling for shrimps with just the horse's head, neck and part of its back showing. I thought this was the horse for me.

All of a sudden we dropped out of our depth and the horse had got to swim. Eddie released the net so that it could swim on, as the net now was acting as an anchor. This is an experience one can do without but all three of us came out of this none the worse but with quite a wetting. I now decided that I would do a trade-in – a straight swap with my horse for his grey gelding. Although he had not seen my horse, he did say that a steadier animal would be more suitable for carting sea-washed turf to the shore. It was therefore arranged that we would meet out in the Bay at a certain time and exchange. I took his horse and he took mine.

I came back and crossed the river Kent, then made on to the Cart Lane crossing, near Guides Farm, up Carter Road at full trot, along Allithwaite Road and through the village. He really could move and when I got him home to

Coming up to eighteen years old in 1950, when my heart was firmly set on a life following the sands.

Flookburgh, dad came out and had a look at him. He said. "He'll be no good to thee mi-lad, maybe for't Derby, but not for shrimping. I can tell thee, t'horse tha swapped fer that were worth ten o' 'im."

The next day I took him out shrimping up to the west side of the Bay in the River Leven, and hardly had time to drop the net from the back of the cart before he was off like a shot. When I asked him to turn he was so quick that the cart almost turned over. After two trawls I decided to call it a day. I had two boxes of shrimps and I barely had time to get the net with the last catch in it onto the cart. When I came out of the water with the net across the back of the cart, that horse just couldn't wait. He set off full ding, trotting not galloping. On rough sand the net was bouncing all over the cart and the shrimps were spilling out from the boxes. I had no time to secure the net or even sort out the shrimps as I could have done with a quieter horse. All I could do was let him go until we reached the shore, then turn him around and secure the net onto the cart before travelling on the road.

I kept him until I received my calling-up papers for the army. Then another fisherman, Jack Butler from Allithwaite, bought him from us, thinking he could tame him, but he never made anything of him. One day after being on the sands, he was turned out of the stable to grass, as were all of the fishermen's horses in the summer months. As he rolled in the field, he twisted his gut and died. It was a very sad end for him to go like that.

I just loved going to the sands and felt that I never wanted to leave them, but now at the age of eighteen I was going to be away from them for a whole two years. Apart from visiting Morecambe and Blackpool, I had never been away from the village, but now I had to report to Blandford in Dorset where I did my training in the Royal Army Training Corps.

CHAPTER THREE

From National Service to Family Life

NATIONAL SERVICE was probably the most horrible experience of my lifetime from day one when I arrived at the camp. It seemed to be miles from anywhere and resembled a prison camp. Along with others I was made to feel about two feet tall or should I say small!. We were bawled at from dawn to dusk and could not do right for doing wrong. I am sure everyone in our squad did his best, but that was never good enough. If you failed to salute an officer and there were many, you were bawled at again. So to get it right we would salute anything that moved, sometimes getting it wrong and made to feel such an idiot. It was hell on earth and I was homesick.

When the weeks of training were finally over, it did become more tolerable when I was posted to a much smaller army camp at Sedgefield in County Durham. This posting became home from home – and so different from the training camp down in Blandford. I now had my own transport and was able to travel home on my motorcycle when I was allowed leave at weekends. Until then it had been stored up at home.

I was lucky to find a place in Sedgefield very close to the Barracks where I could leave my motorcycle and know that it would be perfectly safe. The owner of a small garage was very helpful and gave me a key, so that whatever time I was to use the motorbike, whether it be weekends, or arriving back in the early hours of Monday morning – and it was early – it was nice to know that the proprietor of the garage trusted me.

I never wore a crash helmet and I don't think many people did in those days, but I did wear a very thick flying suit and gloves which kept me nice and warm on the journey in the winter months on the quiet and lonely roads. The route from the barracks took me through the centre of Darlington, then on to Scotch

Corner, where the road turned west for home, via Brough, Kirkby Stephen, Tebay, Kendal and then Flookburgh. This was usually a journey of two to two and a half hours depending on the conditions at the time.

It was always such a lovely feeling to get away from the army routine and arrive home. At eighteen years of age, I was full of life and thought nothing of going fishing, or a late night out with my pals. Coming home, grabbing a bite to eat and then a quick change out of my suit, which at that time was Teddy-boy style, then get clobbered up for the journey back to camp at Sedgefield.

The winter weather was harsh, with sudden frosts which made road surfaces like ice rinks. I had my first spill when my motorcycle shot from under me on a bend in the road. Luckily my bike and me were none the worse for this, but you are just unable to do anything at all about it, as this comes on you so suddenly. I had to finish the journey riding with both feet on the ground as the conditions were so bad and it took me almost twice as long as normal to get back to Sedgefield that unforgettable night, or I should say early morning. But worse was to come.

Two weeks later, feeling tired and having a job to keep my eyes open, I came into dense fog. This was almost in the same area as previously when the road surface became frozen and I again had to travel with both feet on the ground to hold the motorcycle steady. I was creeping along when a bus came from behind and as it passed me I noticed written on the back that it was from Sedgefield. I thought that if I kept close behind the vehicle I would make it a lot easier for myself – but not so.

As the bus took a sharp bend, I must have fallen asleep and rode straight ahead, down an embankment. When I picked myself up, at first all as I could see were the headlights from my motorcycle shining straight up into the air through the fog. Luckily for me, I was none the worse but very shaken up. I was in the middle of nowhere, on my own, with a motorbike half buried in a dense hawthorn hedge and I was now worrying how I was going to get myself back all the way to Sedgefield. I sat on the edge of the grass verge, thinking not of myself, but wondering what could be done about my motorcycle, which I had owned from new for such a short time. Eventually I could hear the sound of a vehicle approaching, so I stood out in the road – not very far because it was thick fog– as I didn't want to miss the opportunity of them seeing me waving my arms for help. It was a lorry and the driver stopped.

T/22620596 Driver Robinson looks far from happy in August 1952.
National Service was probably the most horrible experience of my life.

He was a lovely bloke and helped me a lot. First he dragged my motorcycle out of the hedge and found that it had been badly damaged. He said that no way could I ride it back to camp. I told him where I was stationed and where I lived. He then told me of a garage that he thought would be able to do the repairs needed and said, "Don't worry mi'lad, I will see to that side of it, and then you get in touch with them yourself. I will give you the telephone number." I rang them the very next day and they came and collected it.

The driver of the lorry was only able to take me as far as Scotch Corner, but in no time at all I got a lift in a newspaper delivery van. Although the driver said that he would have me back at the barracks in time he still had his deliveries to do, but that didn't really bother me as long as he got me there.

What a journey! He was a very fast driver and I was sat in the back of the vehicle, which was making me feel sick. But we arrived back at the barracks much earlier than expected and I had time to get myself tidied up for the morning roll call.

As spring came, so did the much better weather and after a few months without my own transport I heard that my motorcycle was ready to be picked up. The only way to get to the garage at Kirkby Stephen was to hitch hike but I made it. There were other hazards as well as the frost and fog, as crossing Bowes Moor was always a nightmare with numerous rabbits running out into the road.

I was at Sedgefield for seven months and then I got a posting nearer home at Fulwood Barracks in Preston. Although I could still use my motorcycle for transport, weekends at home were nothing near as frequent from the new barracks and discipline was tightly ruled. The camp was in two sections, with the Royal Army Service Corps – mostly drivers of vehicles – at one end and the Artillery at the other.

I landed myself quite a cushy number. It was riding a motorcycle, with mail deliveries, outgoing and incoming, to a large Victorian house on the Blackpool road that had been taken over by the Ministry. I was on standby in this office, where the two women typists were very nice civilians in their forties and there was a really pleasant young chap who was also in the RASC. I got to know him quite well and he told me that his name was Fred Burton, from Burton's Biscuits in Blackpool. He travelled in daily in a Riley car. Very posh! Sadly, I was told that his father had died and he was given leave on compassionate grounds.

Whilst I was in the army, my father still fished the Bay for cockles and shrimps and both he and mother followed Barrow market with the fish he caught and home-grown produce. This was still taken to Cark station on a barrow and put in the guard's van to Barrow in Furness station. From here dad wheeled it through the back streets of the town to his pitch on the outside market. There were one or two other families doing the very same thing. This was not easy and they were limited to what they could take on a barrow. The barrows were hand-made with a set of old mangle wheels, a flat bed made of wood and a pair of handles.

On my weekend breaks I found that it was much pleasanter using the train than my motorcycle through the winter months. I also enjoyed the long walk from the station at Preston, looking in most of the shop windows, then past the prison and up Deepdale road, passing the famous football grounds and eventually reaching the barracks.

Our company, the RASC, was not allowed to use the main entrance as this was for the infantry. The RASC had its own entrance around the other side, but when I had to leave the barracks by army motorcycle on duty, I just simply rode through the main gate and never ever got pulled up.

Most sergeant majors in the army had a frightening reputation whilst on duty. They came over with a very loud voice and seemed to put the fear of god into the squaddies. This was the case at Fulwood Barracks, but not for me. The sergeant major didn't have long to serve in the army before his retirement. He always coughed a heck of a lot and, although he smoked cigarettes, they were special ones with no nicotine. These gave him ease from this cough and so he had never to be without them. I could get these for him in Preston but only in certain shops. He was forever giving me money to bring him these special cigarettes. Now I knew why I never ever got pulled up on the army motorcycle when using the main entrance – 'a friend in need is a friend indeed!'

I could hardly believe the change in his character when he needed his cigarettes. It was during one of these trips that I noticed a garage on the roadside with vans and motorcars marked up for sale. I thought of my parents, pushing the barrow loaded up with fish and vegetables for the market. So one day I decided to stop at this garage and look at what they had for sale, find out the prices they were asking and see if they had a vehicle suitable for my parents.

At the weekend I was able to travel home and let my parents know what I had been doing. They had some very good news for me that was quite exciting. Dad's brother, Maurice, and his wife Muriel, with daughter Jennifer, had decided to sell their houses in almost an acre of land and they had given my parents the first choice of buying the property. This was a chance not to be missed – so they went for it. My sister Jean was at home but working at the carpet factory in Kendal and travelling each day by bus. She was a worker and a jolly good help to my parents.

My time in the army didn't have long to go, so I told mum and dad that I had been to a garage in Preston looking at the prices of second hand cars. They felt the idea was a good one, but right now with the expense of moving house they thought it best to wait a while.

The next time I came home for the weekend I travelled on the train. I had decided that to return to Preston I would now, once again, use my motorcycle, but did not tell my parents what I intended to do. The next time I had visited the garage they had had a Bedford van for sale. It looked in good condition and would suit my parents and make life much easier for them, so I asked the boss or salesman – I think he was both – if it would be possible to put my motorcycle towards an exchange deal. After he gave it the once-over we fixed a price to be paid. The boss seemed a genuine person and made it very easy for me to agree the payment.

It was arranged that dad would travel down from Cark station to Preston by train and I would meet him. We would then go on my motorcycle to the garage in Blackpool Road, which was not very far from the station. He was pleased when he saw the van and, after looking it over, my motorcycle was taken towards the payment and dad paid the man the rest. Dad had no driving licence, although he had been driving vehicles all of his time in the army, but it had either been lost or had expired.

I do not know quite what we did about insurance for the van but I remember driving it back to Grange and putting it in the garage. This was at the weekend and I had to be back at Fulwood Barracks for early Monday morning. Once every week I was asked if I would go into town to pick up driving licences for the new recruits in the camp. The building and offices were opposite the railway station and at that time it was the main place to obtain your driving licence. When I mentioned to them that dad didn't have a licence, the two secretaries in the office in the barracks did us a great favour and wrote dad's details down. When I was asked to go and pick up the new licences at the licence centre, I found when I got back to the barracks that among all the others was one for my father. Dad was well pleased. He and mother would now find market days much easier and could also take much more produce in the van.

HARD TIMES

I could not wait for those two long years of National Service to pass and get back to my family and friends and the beloved sands. We now had to look out for another horse to enable me to fish along with my father and other fishermen who followed the sands for a living. We were lucky.

Harry Shaw, a fisherman from just across the road where we lived, had this really good horse – a piebald – but he could not make up his mind about selling it. One day he would talk about selling and the very next day he would have changed his mind, but eventually dad persuaded him to sell and we jumped at the chance and bought it. This horse had a name for being good at shrimping and, luckily for us, other fishermen did not know that it was for sale. It could wade, pulling a cart with a net dragging behind for shrimps, with just its head, neck and part of its back showing out of the water, and never got excited. A horse like this one – reliable and able to bring you out of sticky situations – was worth its weight in gold.

We now had two horses and fished the Bay according to the tides, both through the night and during the day. Cockle fishing was the main source of our livelihood as there is no 'closed season', so we could gather them both winter and summer. Although the Bay is so vast and cockle beds can lie over such huge areas, in 1962 the harsh winter frosts decimated the cockle stocks and they did not recover until the 1970s. These were hard times and I was desperate to find a job of any kind.

A fishing pal of mine, Brian Shaw of Flookburgh, rang me up to tell me that Listers factory in Barrow in Furness were advertising for workers. We rang up and were accepted. We had to clock in every morning and when you finished in the evening. I only lasted for one week! What an environment in which to work. The noise was continually deafening and it was so hot and worse still, no-one ever spoke a word to either me or Brian. I gave in my notice and could not wait for the week to end and to look for a job outside in the fresh air, if possible.

I then heard that a local character, George Broadhust, was looking for labourers to work on the site of the new Heysham Power Station. I got in touch with George, whom I had known well, and he told me he had got a contract with a firm on the Heysham site digging trenches and laying electricity cables, and that I could join his team of local lads on the Monday. George lived in the village of Cartmel and suggested that I pick him up early Monday morning to arrive at Heysham just as it was getting light. The weather was cold, with snow and ice still around, and as we were to dig trenches manually, with picks and shovels, it was hard work. But it was a job and it was outside, so I gave it a go till the spring arrived. I then decided to give in my notice as it was time to start fishing again.

In the early 1960s I was involved in the Morecambe Bay Barrage Survey, which proved to be a very interesting and rewarding two years. In his book *Grange over Sands: The story of a Gentle Township* (1969), the late W E Swale, who was a great friend of ours, describes the work of the Survey and the problems of the task in which I became so closely involved.

Towns north of a line from Hest Bank to Ulverston faced the possible construction of a barrage, which would drastically alter their physical surroundings. The object of the original scheme was merely to carry a railway line running to Carlisle and Scotland, but since then other objectives have included a shorter rail and road route to Barrow along the top of the dam, a source of cooling water for electricity power stations, land reclamation and, above all, water storage. If it did nothing else, the 'feasibility study' aroused a great interest and was a minor source of local employment. Estimated to cost around £500,000, it proceeded under the overall direction of the Water Resources Board in Reading. The combined skill of a number of specialist firms was called upon so that every conceivable aspect of a complex problem could be exhaustively examined.

Consulting engineers dealt with constructional work, surveyors made aerial and hydrographical observations, and experts in soil mechanics sunk over thirty-five boreholes reaching depths of over 300 feet. A scale model was made of the waters and shores of Morecambe Bay with the aim that simulated tides would indicate the long-term effects of the barrage as far down as Barrow harbour.

All those involved must have read accounts of the extraordinary high tide of 27 December 1857, which exceeded by twelve feet anything ever recorded before or since. There was also the great gale of 27 February 1903, when, in the early hours of the morning, the down mail train was blown over as it was crossing Leven viaduct, fortunately without loss of life. These incidents prove that Morecambe Bay will not be easily tamed.

There has been talk now for some time with plans to build a bridge across the Bay connecting Barrow and Heysham. The state of the art structure with wind turbines above it and hydro turbines below is the brainchild of Kendal based businessman, David Brockbank. He claims that completion of the link would open up the whole of the west coast of Cumbria to people from the area and further afield.

In 1972, after five years of study of a proposed barrage, the Water Resources Board concluded that Morecambe Bay could be used for freshwater storage but the idea was shelved as being too costly. All this is now in the past – but not forgotten. Sometime in the future a bridge could become a reality, but as long as the tides still ebb and flow into the Bay, my job as guide over the sands will be secure.

Following my work on the Barrage Survey, I received a request from the Electricity Board asking if I would meet up with officials at Askam in Furness. The idea was for us to walk across the Duddon Sands and for me to give an opinion on whether they were safe enough to transport heavy machinery.

An electricity cable was to be taken part way across the estuary from the Millom side by boat. The cable was on huge drums and the boat could only operate on the high tides. The plan was for the boat to run aground shortly after crossing the river area and the deeper section of the estuary, and then release the huge drums of cables down onto the sands. Then, if the sands were safe enough, large caterpillar machines were to travel out from the Askam side of the estuary and drag the cable the rest of the way.

After meeting up with the officials and walking across the estuary as far as the River Duddon, I found the sands safe enough to take the weight of these machines. As we walked back over the way we came, I was thanked for my services and did not think that I would hear from them again, but I did – years later.

Seemingly, they told me by letter, they had a fault in the cable and would I meet up with them again at the same place at Askam? I did, and a member of their team had this hand-operated object – something like a metal detector. We walked slowly over the sands, with this one person operating whatever it was all the way to the River Duddon, which at this time was running close to the old jetty at Millom. No fault was found in this section, so we returned to the shore at Askam. I was thanked, once again for my assistance, and they said that they would drive round the estuary to Millom and test the short length from the shore. This is where they found the fault and wrote and told me so.

I had not been onto those sands for years, but I remember quite clearly a group of Flookburgh fishermen cockling on the Duddon estuary and I was out there with them when I was a very young lad.

OLIVE – AND HER FOUR CHILDREN

Most of the fishing families had a market garden or a smallholding as a sideline for when there was a lull in fishing, and they would also follow the markets either in Barrow or Kendal. Our own market garden was doing well and we needed some help with the weeding. One lad called Bill, who was the eldest son of one of the men I had known in the Flookburgh Band a few years earlier, seemed the sort of lad we wanted. His father had died quite recently and his mother was only too glad for the lad to earn a bit of spare cash. So Bill came along after school and at weekends to work with us in the garden – and a good help he was too. He would turn his hand to anything, helping dad to load the van ready for the market, weeding and transplanting. We always grew a large bed of lettuce, which we tried to get ready early to sell at the best prices in the market.

As we had three greenhouses, all 60ft by 16ft, we were able to grow earlier crops for the Easter market, providing we trenched in a good load of farmyard manure. When the first crops were cleared we followed them with tomatoes and quite a lot of bedding plants, but for these we had to have a little heat to start them off. The heating came from a cast-iron coke stove, which once the coke got really red hot kept its heat all through the night. This gave the plants a good start and then they were ready to be pricked out into boxes to grow on ready for sale on the Barrow open market.

As well as market gardening, I was continuing to follow the sands at all times of the day and night according to the tides. Bill was such a sharp but steady and reliable lad that I asked him if he would come out on the sands with me. This idea really appealed to him and he jumped at the opportunity. He soon got used to handling the horse and cart, taking to the work as if he was born to it.

Eventually, Bill persuaded me to buy an old David Brown Cropmaster TVO tractor. There was a small tank of petrol for starting, then as the engine warmed up you turned over to paraffin TVO. If you turned over too soon the engine used to splutter like mad. I was not too keen at first, thinking that this old tractor was not going to be as reliable as my horse and cart, but later we got more used to its ways and learnt to trust it, venturing out onto the sands as far as the cockle beds. We didn't pull a trailer and instead built a wooden platform at the back of the tractor, which would carry a couple of hundredweight or so of cockles and the gear needed at the time. We were often out over the sands and at the cockle beds as dawn was breaking. In summer it was a grand feeling coming home across the marsh with the smell of the summer hay wafting over from the distant meadow. We would hear the bellowing cows as the early rising farmer took his herd in for milking.

As we came away from the sands and onto the mile long straight road leading to the village, the only noise we could hear was from the old rumbling tractor. Coming through the village, the billowing smoke from the cottage chimneys showed us that people were rising, ready to start their daily routine. We put the tractor away after unloading the cockles and felt a glow of satisfaction that we had done so well, so early in the morning, before most people had even thought of getting out of their beds.

I had done no more than pass the time of day with Bill's mother up to this time, though I knew something of the family from him. One evening when we had been out after a late tide, I took Bill back to his home and he asked his mother whether I could come in for a cup of tea. That was the beginning of a lasting relationship. Bill's mother, Olive Nickson, had four children. Bill was the eldest and then came Robert, a quiet lad. Diane was a very pretty little girl with blonde hair – the image of her mother – and then Paul, the baby who was just over a year old. My visits, like the rest of my life, were governed by the tides and this meant that sometimes I didn't see Olive for several days on end.

Out there on the sands, going across the miles, I thought about the future, and

Olive and I were married at St John the Baptist church in Flookburgh on 30 October 1961.

Our daughter Jean, born in January 1963, was introduced to animals at an early age.
Young Bill is on the left and I am keeping a watchful eye.

Opposite: A later photograph of Jean cockling in the Bay with basket and cramb. (Peter
Cherry)

wondered if it was too soon to ask Olive if she had ever thought of marrying again. I decided not to be in such a hurry and so my visits went on as usual, just taking Bill home and perhaps staying for a bit of supper and watching television for an hour or so. I would often have baby Paul on my knee while his mother got some supper ready for us all and little Diane would sit by my side chattering away as children do. The pattern of my days was changing. I spent as much time as work would let me with Olive and her family and we came to know each other very well.

My sister Jean was now married to Tony Sawrey, a farmer's son from Great Urswick, near Ulverston, and living in a modern caravan on land close to the farmhouse. Jean and I were always best of friends and very close, so I thought I would have a ride through to see them. I wanted to tell them that I had fallen in love with the girl I wished to marry and that she was a small, blonde, very good looking, gentle, quietly spoken lass called Olive. She was also a widow with four small children. Naturally, my parents were very worried, as I was young and they thought that it was a lot for their only son – on whom they doted – to take on. However, I was determined to marry Olive, come what may, so sister Jean and Tony said, "Go for it!"

We had known each other now for nearly two years and I felt that all the family had accepted me, so I was fairly sure what her answer would be. She thought that we should wait a while longer to make absolutely certain of our feelings for each other, so it was not until 30 October 1961 that we had our quiet wedding at St. John the Baptist church in Flookburgh. The service was conducted by the Reverend Fowler. Afterwards, Olive and I, Jean and Tony drove to the Swan Hotel at Newby Bridge for a lovely meal and the children and grandparents all had a wonderful party at home. For the next two years we lived at the house that Olive had been occupying with her family. The children were delightful and my family grew to love Olive and her children, Bill, Robert, Diane and Paul. Later, when Bill left school, he came to work with me and my father, who we always called Granddad Rob. Young Bill started going to the Barrow market with my parents and found he was a born trader, and it was here he met his future wife Jackie.

On 3 January 1963 our daughter Jean was born, which added to our happiness. Marrying Olive was the best thing I ever did. We have now been married for forty-seven years and have been very happy. Olive has been a great help to me in my work, especially with her lovely illustrations that she has done in my books. We are a great partnership and are looking forward to celebrating our Golden Wedding anniversary.

CHAPTER FOUR

Sands Guide

ALTHOUGH I LIVED in Flookburgh and followed the sands regularly, neither Olive nor I had ever heard of the walks across Morecambe Bay. One day out on the sands, miles out from the shore, Bill and I were hard at work gathering cockles, when in the distance we could just make out what looked like a person heading straight towards us. Bill was surprised and said to me, "Who would think of walking out on the sands, all this way, unless it is someone who knows what he is doing?" As the person got nearer, I knew who it was. It was the North Western Sea Fishery Officer, Gren Harrison.

He was the law officer – the policeman of the sands – and occasionally he would turn up out of the blue and inspect the size of cockles we were gathering. He was a well-built chap and very strong. He always wore a dark uniform, similar to that of a naval officer and thigh boots. He was always very fair with the local fishermen as some of them did not always toe the line, but I always got on well with him. Bill and I were just about to make ready for home, both feeling tired after working non-stop for about four hours. The filled cockle bags weighed all of a hundredweight and needed the two of us, one each side of the bag, to lift them onto the cart after we had made it easier by taking out the 'eck' (that's the tailboard). He came forward and offered to help, lifting them clean over the back of the cart without even taking down the 'eck' and without any effort at all. He was amazing and had the strength of two men.

As we moved away from the cockle beds making for home, Gren walked alongside all the way and chatted to us. He mentioned that the Sands Guide at Grange, Mr Burrow (nicknamed Buff), was retiring and he thought I would be a likely candidate for the job. If I was at all interested I would have to apply in writing and if so he would call and give me the address.

When we arrived back at the stable, the cockles were unloaded and the horse unyoked, put in his stall and given a feed of oats. Staying out on the sands for hours on end gives one an appetite and Olive – a really good cook – always had

a splendid meal ready for us. I told her what Gren had said to me about the Guide's job becoming available at Grange. Although we were happy as we were, living in Ravenstown, she said she would go along with whatever I should decide. So I did as Gren suggested and applied in writing, and was asked to go for an interview before finally being chosen as 'The Queen's Guide to the Kent Sands of Morecambe Bay'. That was in October 1963.

There are two officially appointed Sands Guides, one for each side of the Bay. The River Kent is my responsibility, while the other present Guide, Raymond Porter, is responsible for the Leven Sands. Although local tradition has it that the Guides were in existence in the time of King John, there is no supporting evidence. The office of Guide to the Kent Sands may have been instituted by the Prior of Cartmel – the religious house nearest to the sands – in the fourteenth century, but there are no records to be found of Guides before the reign of Henry VIII.

The salaries of both Guides are secured from the revenues of the Duchy of Lancaster, although by the Charitable Acts of 1853 and 1869 they passed under the control of the Charity Commissioners, with the Chancellor of the Duchy as one of the trustees. In 1882 the Chancellor was discharged from this responsibility and three local trustees were appointed to administer the charity. This arrangement is still in force.

The Guide's salary is £15 per year, paid annually after rent has been deducted. Obviously it is not a full-time job and a living has to be made, mostly from fishing the Bay. Rates have to be paid on Guides Farm, which goes with the job, but good use can be made of the adjoining land with the outbuildings. Very little had been done to improve the property over the years as this was the responsibility of the trustees, who did tell us at the time that the property needed a lot doing to it.

I was busy cockling out in the Bay, as seen here, when a chance encounter led me to apply for the post of Guide to the Kent Sands. (Peter Cherry)

We moved into Guides Farm in October 1963, when there was no mains electricity and only some very primitive gas lighting. (Peter Cherry)

GUIDES FARM

We moved to Guides Farm in early October 1963 and found we had a lot to do to make ourselves comfortable. We had to work night and day, as it was our busiest time for the shrimping. At this stage we were still boiling our shrimps at dad's cottage as there was no suitable place at Guides Farm. One of the biggest drawbacks was that there was no electricity laid on at the farm. There were gas lights, but only in the living room and the kitchen. These must have been as old as the hills because the light from them was so dull and poor that it was not even as good as the glow from a candle.

We didn't seem to mind as we were so happy, but now Olive had extra burdens piled upon her, with washing, cooking and ironing for five children and a husband and no washing machine, electric iron or vacuum cleaner. We could not use our cooker or television – not that we ever had time for TV. It was hard, but we were willing to put up with these things - for a time at least.

We worked day and night once we had moved into Guides Farm as it was a busy time for fishing. Here I am tending to the nets on the shore close to the farm.

With everyone doing their bit to help us, we eventually made headway. In the outbuilding next to the house was an old set pot – a cast iron washing boiler with a coal-fired grate. This hadn't been used for years by the looks of it. So Bill and I gave it a good clean up and renewed the grate and then we used it for boiling and washing all the clothes. Luckily we had an ancient mangle that squeezed the wet clothes between wooden rollers, which got rid of the surplus water. Then we hung them out to dry on the washing line that I had put up in the orchard.

One day, after pegging out the washing on the line, I opened the front door to see someone helping himself to our washing from the line. At first glance I thought it was one of us, but looking round I saw that the whole family were in the living room. I ran up the pathway towards the orchard and this young chap, in a red jumper, took off as fast as his legs would carry him. He cleared the small hedge, from the orchard into the back field, in one leap. He flew and there was just no way I could have kept pace with him, so he got well away. The incident was reported to the police but the culprit was never found. It was mainly baby clothes that went missing, so it seemed that someone was far worse off than us.

Decorating was a task we all shared, but as it was so late on in the year the days were short and it came dark just after teatime, which didn't help us in any way.

We used two oil lamps with mantles and these gave us a much better light than the gas in the living room, although as they hung from the low beams I was forever banging my head on them. Candles were used to light us up to bed and we were always very careful with them, because the house was so very old. Many a time, getting up in the middle of the night to go out shrimping, I found out how much I missed the electricity. I had to use a torch, which I kept by my bedside, to see the time. I couldn't be fiddling about with matches in the middle of the night. I got up and went downstairs, and then had to light a primus stove, which we had borrowed from Gren Harrison, before I could have a cup of tea. This was really taking us back to the olden days, with all the disadvantages.

The house has an interesting history. It is said that Oliver Cromwell once slept here and as I made my way down the creaking stairs in the very early hours, with the sound of the winter winds howling around, I could almost feel like he was there. I would often think about how people dressed, so many centuries ago, and sometimes even imagine that our old house was haunted. At one time, long ago, the upper floor was one big room. Travellers crossing the sands and arriving late in the evening, tired and weary from the long journey, often very wet and cold, could come into Guides Farm and get a few hours rest and a drink of something to warm them up, as the house had been granted a licence to sell ale. This, in those days, augmented the Guide's income. I could just imagine a room full of weary travellers, drinking ale and romancing about their journey across those

Guides Farm nestles close to the shoreline on the right-hand edge of this photograph. This was the view that would be seen by weary travellers in former times as they completed the crossing of the Bay. (Peter Cherry)

treacherous sands.

When Guides Farm was built, and it is said to be around seven or eight hundred years old, the very high tides would have come right up into the house. There was no embankment there to stop them until the railway came and an embankment was built along the coast. We found that all the ground floors sloped towards the shore, so the living rooms, with the old blue stone flag floors, could easily have been swilled out after such happenings. Oddly enough, there was a deep step into the kitchen, and the ceiling was so low that there was hardly enough headroom for anyone of my height, almost six feet, to stand upright. So we decided to dig up the floor and bring it level with that of the living room, as it was a danger in the poor light. Under the floor we found good clean sand and cockle shells, so it must have been tidal ground at some time before being built on.

The winter seemed long, and as time passed we were looking forward to the day when we could have electricity brought to the house. We had been using oil

lamps and candles for almost six months, although it seemed much longer. We had written to the trustees, who had appointed me, to see if it would be possible to have electricity installed. They gave us the go ahead, although we had to foot the bill in the first place. The money was eventually paid back to us. We had to apply to the Electricity Board and soon things got moving. A gang of twelve men arrived to dig along the lane to Guides Farm. With no mechanical means this was hard labour, with picks and shovels digging through solid limestone.

All was excitement when in February 1964 the work was finished and in March the electric was turned on. This changed all our lives, but none so much as that of Olive. The washer, fridge and cooker were soon fixed up in the kitchen and made life really worth living again when it came to all the jobs she had to do for the whole family. The fearsome shadows that had scared us for the last six months on the creaking staircase all vanished and going to bed was no longer a nightmare. Had we all been imagining those sinister figures lurking in corners?

The click of a switch and they just disappeared. Even so, when I got up during the night to go to my nets, I would step out onto the old creaking landing and sometimes thought that I saw a figure standing there before me. It was eerie and I used to say to myself that this cannot be, but I was always glad to switch on the light!

We were very pleased with the progress we had made and everything ran smoothly for several months. Then came a setback. As the house was so old, it had no damp course. Now all our hard work wallpapering, of which we were so proud, was wasted. Suddenly, piece

The flower-rich hay meadows of Guides Farm benefit from the maritime climate of Grange, which has the highest spring temperatures in the north of England. (Peter Cherry)

by piece the paper started coming away from the walls. We realised just how damp they were and decided to strip off all the old plaster and start again from rock bottom, making a really good job of it and plastering afresh.

One night we were sitting round a cheerful log fire when all at once there was a deafening roar. You would have thought a bomb had just dropped on the house. We rushed to open the sitting room door and Olive was the first to see the mess. All the plaster we had put on had left the walls and was spread all over the carpet. There was dust and plaster everywhere and Olive was in tears. "Never mind love," I said, "We will soon have it cleared up and then we will see what can be done."

We decided that if we couldn't cure the damp we would just have to hide it, so our son Robert, who was serving his apprenticeship as a joiner with Jim Saunders, made battens on which he fastened hardboard and we then papered over it. After this treatment the sitting room looked nice and cosy, but even then some signs of damp would show when there was heavy rain. Eventually we put tarred paper under the wallpaper on the walls of the ground floor rooms. This helped to stop the discoloration to some extent, although it did not prevent the dampness.

We had worse to come. Almost a year after this happened we had an even greater shock. One evening Olive was getting the children ready for bed. I had already gone upstairs, as I had to be out on the sands at four o'clock the next morning. I was just dozing off when I heard her shouting, "Ced, Ced, come quick there's a flood!."

It had rained quite heavily for a few hours and as I stepped down from the bedroom onto the landing I found myself ankle deep in water, which was running down the stairs like a waterfall. Olive was already lifting the lino from the living room floor. As the floor sloped down towards the front door, the water was running out like a river. It bubbled up through the bottom stair as if there was a spring underneath.

Upstairs in the bathroom the lino was afloat. There was water seeping into the sitting room and we had to move all the furniture and take up the carpet, which later had to go away to be dried. Water was running through the wall of the kitchen and had built up to about a foot deep outside the window. What a job we had to try to get everything out – there was little sleep for any of us that night!

The house is built into the hillside on limestone, with earth reaching up to the foot of the kitchen window, and there is a door on the first floor landing level with the ground outside. So it was not surprising that in really heavy rain, such as we had that day, the water should have built up sufficiently to flood the house. The trustees decided that the only way to prevent this from happening again would be to have the earth removed from most of the back wall and to have it all cemented. This was done and fortunately it proved very effective.

The setting of Guides Farm is of special interest. It is situated on an east-facing slope overlooking Morecambe Bay and there are a number of valuable habitats on the farm. Their importance is heightened by the fact that they are present over carboniferous limestone with a distinct maritime climate influence, with Grange having the highest spring temperatures in the North of England. There are two hay meadows, two pastures, tall multi-species (and presumably old) hedges, limestone dry stone walls and some small areas of scrub.

There is one very busy footpath along the bottom of the meadows, which gives passers-by an excellent view of them, especially when they are in full flower in June or July. At each end of the footpath there is a kissing gate, which stops the cattle from escaping.

The land is designated as an "important open area" in the South Lakeland District Council's local plan and is part of the Grange over Sands Conservation Area. There is scope for the provision of some interpretation of the land, its historic associations and how it needs to be managed by traditional farming practices to maintain its wildlife and beauty.

This is especially important since there is a heavy use by local people and visitors alike of the public footpath running along the coast as it does from Grange over Sands to Kent's Bank. Whilst there is no pressure for developing the land for housing at the present time, the Countryside Stewardship Scheme and associated grant aid would go a long way to enhancing its status.

Crossing the River Kent near the causeway on an early cross-Bay walk in 1964.

CROSS-BAY WALKS

My appointment as Guide at a fairly young age seemed to have aroused some interest further afield as we had a visit from a journalist, who drove up all the way from London to take part on one of my first walks and take pictures for the *Geographical Magazine*. His name was Axel Poignent.

We allowed him to park his camper van in the yard at the farm and the following day I organised a walk across the Bay to Hest Bank. At that time the most suitable place to start the walk was from Grange over Sands railway station, under the subway and down the causeway and then out onto the sands. The River Kent was running only a short distance out from the station and on this particular walk there were only a handful of walkers. There had been very little publicity and in those days the walks were hardly known. It took our small party just over three hours, crossing the rivers Kent and Keer with no difficulty. Coming onto the shore at Hest Bank there were a few remarks by some of the walkers about feeling tired, but everyone said how much they had enjoyed this unique experience and would like to come again sometime.

One of the more unusual early trips I made across the Bay was when the Roundhead Association asked for my help as they wished to cross the sands with their army. This was a most interesting and picturesque walk or march, as all the people were dressed in appropriate costumes and kept in formation. On the far side of the Bay at White Creek the Cavaliers were waiting – also in full dress – and as the Roundheads drew near a cannon was fired. This was a signal for a pitched battle to begin. It was a most beautiful day and the River Kent was only about knee deep as we crossed. The battle lasted for about half an hour – a much shorter affair than when the real Roundheads were about in this area so many centuries ago.

I find all of my walks interesting, but these two stand out as being the most memorable in those early years.

Following these walks I found that it would have been much easier starting from this side of the Bay but not feasible owing to the time scale between the tides. Having to start from the opposite side of the Bay was a bit of a problem. A walk across the Bay cannot just happen and a lot of planning had to be done the day before the organised event with the public. Sands, rivers, dykes and gullies had to be examined and a safe and shallow route marked out with laurel bushes. The walks varied in distance according to the movement of the River Kent, but would take at least three hours to cover the eight or nine miles.

Olive has always kept an eye on me whilst out there on my own, as I have a very powerful telescope, essential for the work I do out in the Bay. It is an ex-naval prismatic monocular gun-sighting telescope, made of brass and weighing fifteen and a half pounds. I would always tell Olive, before setting out, the approximate times at which I would be in certain places so that she would know in which direction to look. One thing absolutely certain was that being out in the Bay for several hours at a time gave me such an appetite and Olive always had a good meal waiting for me when I arrived home.

The Bay offers much more to people than just a walk across from one side to the other. It can be educational, especially to groups of youngsters as there are many interesting things to be seen and learned from such a visit, and what could be more exciting than to undertake the adventure for the first time.

A MEMORABLE WALK

I had an enquiry for a walk across the Bay with a school party of thirty children and their teachers. This had aroused quite an interest, so I arranged a Saturday morning in August for them and they all arrived and gathered on the beach at Hest Bank. The children were all excited at the prospect of crossing the Bay on foot with the Sands Guide leading them. I was there in time, waiting for them, bare-footed and wearing blue jeans, with shirt sleeves rolled up, a whistle on a

Fishing the fluke out in the Bay. Children on cross-Bay walks often think the nets are 'some form of fence'. (Peter Cherry)

string around my neck and carrying a staff.

Small children are always inquisitive and ask lots of questions – and I like this to happen. "What's the whistle for, mister?" "Why do you have that big stick?" "How far is it to the river?" "Shall we be able to swim?" "Is there any quicksand?" These and many more questions are fired at me most of the time by children, almost disbelieving that they are really out there in Morecambe Bay on a journey they will never forget. A vast expanse of what appears to be featureless sands, sandbanks and gullies left behind by the receding tide exerts a strange magnetic effect upon most youngsters. Boys and girls alike just love splashing alarmingly through the dykes and gullies and then out onto clean firm sand.

On this occasion the sun was beating down on us as bold as brass and we could scarcely bear to look into it. It was like a sheet of silver as it shone on the water. We came across a net that had been set by a Flookburgh fisherman to catch the white fluke or flounder. At first sight the children thought that it looked like some sort of a fence, but when they got much nearer I explained to them that this was the method used by the fishermen of the Bay. The net was full of flukes and the excitement rose as the children could see lots entangled up in the meshes with many more – unseen to a stranger – partly buried in the sand. Each child wanted to take home some fish from the net, but I had to explain that this was not possible. Time and money had been spent by the fisherman who owned the net and he would not be at all pleased if he suddenly turned up and found us taking away his fish.

I found it hard to keep these inquisitive youngsters at bay when we suddenly saw something moving and making a splash about halfway along the net where it was set through a dyke. This was found to be a large skate and I started to shake it free from the bag of the net and release it into the water. They all gathered round and one said, "Ooh! That's a stingray, aren't you brave, mister! If that had stung you, you would have been dead by now."

We all watched this large fish take to the water almost as a bird takes to the air, with its huge fins beating up and down. Now and again they showed above the surface like large wings as the fish propelled its way down the dyke and into deeper water. I explained to them that this rarely happens these days, as this type of fish normally frequents deeper waters around stony scars and mussel beds and does not usually come up this far into the upper reaches of the Bay.

We now had to move on towards the River Kent and all the children and their

A fluke is disentangled from a net and carefully placed in a cockle basket.
(Peter Cherry)

teachers showed extreme interest in all we were seeing. The weather forecast had been good and as we approached the river, I made a point of telling them that we were going to have a good crossing. As there was little or no fresh water in the river so there should be no problems. As we made our way into the river most of them started splashing one another with delight. The water temperature was lovely and warm like that of their bathwater.

One or two of them squirmed uneasily as they trod on a fluke in the riverbed. The Kent was very wide but shallow. Crossing a wide expanse of water is much more tiring than walking on the sands, but I did not hear anyone complain. As we reached the other side of the river and stepped out onto the reasonably dry sand, the Bay looked at its best with clear views in every direction.

A few youngsters came running back to me to tell me they had seen lots of tiny bubbles all over the sand and wanted to know what was happening. They were not bubbles but small jellyfish in their hundreds – transparent, almost colourless and about the size of a small gooseberry. I explained that these come up into the Bay in hot weather in great numbers, usually June to August and that they are non-stinging and the local fishermen call them 'Jujubes'.

One child asked me, "Are there anymore jellyfish in the Bay – any large ones?"

"Oh yes," was my reply, "And if we are lucky we may even come across one or two before long."

Now they were really interested and started looking to see what they could find. The children had been collecting small shells as they walked across the sands to take back home. These were small bivalves, known as 'Hen Pennies' by the local fishermen. They come in three colours – blue, pink and white – and are a valuable food source for the birdlife and the fluke, which come up into the Bay on the rising tides and feed out on the sandbanks. The children picked up quite an assortment of cockle shells as well as larger whitish shells of the clam and a few whelks.

Now something different was spotted just ahead and one or two of the more inquisitive children ran on ahead to investigate the find. This was just what I had been hoping for to complete the day out. A massive jellyfish, almost the size of a dustbin lid, was lying on the sand and looked to be very much alive.

I blew my whistle at this point to attract their attention and asked them to gather round, but not too near so that everyone could have a clear view of this fine specimen, which I estimated to be about three feet across and probably weighing about forty pounds. I gathered my hands carefully around both edges of the jellyfish's skirt and held it slightly aloft so that everyone could see the tentacles that hung down almost like a chandelier. They were all amazed, staring goggle-eyed at this monster jellyfish, almost transparent and thinking it should have stung the daylights out of me.

Children pick up cockle shells on the walks and like to know all about cockling. Here I
have been using a 'jumbo' and my son-in-law Chris Jackson has raked the cockles into a
riddle. He is now emptying them into a wastepaper basket, deputising for the cockle
basket that had been forgotten! (Peter Cherry)

Cockling can often be bitterly cold. You can almost feel the winter weather in this scene out in the Bay. (Peter Cherry)

I could only hold it up for a few seconds, owing to the weight and slipperiness of the thing. I explained to them that this type was harmless, but there is another species of jellyfish that can give you a very nasty sting. It was not usually found as large as this one and had a brown decorative frill around the edge of the dome. I have accidentally been stung by this kind of jellyfish while fishing my nets. It really hurts as the sting is about ten times stronger than that of a nettle.

As we moved on towards the shore at Kents Bank, the group was now much quieter than when we set out. As I stood looking back over the Bay, one young girl, who had very little to say when we were out on the sands, came alongside me and said "I know what I'm going to do when I get home."

"What's that?" I asked.

"Well," she said, "I think I will go straight upstairs to bed. I've never been so tired in all my life!"

Her little pal was not so lucky. She said, "When I get home, I've got to take our dog out for a walk."

I could have listened to these children for hours. Some were weary from their experience, whilst others were still full of themselves. This particular walk, although one of many, gave me memories I shall treasure for a long, long time.

Leaving the shore for their transport home, they all shouted. "Thank you, Mr Robinson." I then sat down on one of the seats on the shore to put my shoes on, and looked back over the sands of the magical Morecambe Bay.

BEATING THE BOUNDS

In 1977 I was involved when an ancient ceremony called 'beating the bounds' was revived at Silverdale to crown the Silver Jubilee celebrations. As the original parish boundary was several miles in length, over some difficult ground and included a stretch of Morecambe Bay, it was decided to spread the event over two days. The most difficult part was tackled on the Saturday and included a journey along the Kent channel in an inflatable rubber dinghy. Many supporters followed us for most of the way, and they got quite a wetting. I was asked to go along to make sure the party kept out of the dangerous areas.

The organisers tried to follow the exact route and ceremonial recorded in the history books, with the symbolic blessing of the four triangular piles of boundary stones. The seaward boundary of the parish extends from the county wall beyond the Cove, in a straight line across the Bay towards Guides Farm at Grange over Sands, until it reaches the Kent Channel. It then runs south along mid-channel until it is intersected by a line drawn from Pigeon Cote Lane on the Humphrey Head side of the Bay and finally eastwards towards Bardswell. There is one unusual feature of the 'bounds' in that the western boundary runs down the centre of the Kent channel. As the channel sometimes moves from one side of the Bay to the other, so the Silverdale bounds move too.

Enjoyable as was the walk, there were moments in the Kent channel when the flow was so swift that it was running in 'gilimers' (a dialect word meaning that the channel is like rapids in a river). We thought that at any moment the dinghy would overturn, but we made it 'on the line' according to plan. Those who followed us watched from the edge of the channel and remarked that it made them dizzy to see us battling our way through the rough waters. The party also became fearful on the homeward journey when, on the turn of the tide, they were crossing gullies knee-deep in water with sand moving beneath our feet. They were all thankful when we reached the safety of the shore once again and our feet were once more on solid earth.

OTHER WALKS

In 2006 I led a walk across the Duddon estuary from Askam to Millom and I was asked to do so again in 2009. It is not easy making these decisions, as my walks over the sands are always popular, but it represents a nice change of scenery and a different river.

Another estuary and another time, I accompanied two journalists across the Ribble estuary from Southport to Lytham St. Annes. It was an experience that I enjoyed, but nothing compared to our famous Morecambe Bay. It has no equal.

PEN TO PAPER

It would have been the last thought in my mind to have to put pen to paper and write a book of my experiences of life as a fisherman and Queen's Guide over the Kent Sands. Then I met Eric Swale, a retired engineer from Manchester, who with his lovely wife retired to Grange over Sands. After several visits to Guides Farm and lots of Olive's lovely cups of tea, he said that I was giving away far too much information about the sands and my job as Guide to every journalist that came along, so why not put all that I knew down on paper and start writing a book.

I took Eric's advice and went ahead. My only previous writing experience was answering letters of enquiry about the cross-Bay walk. But I was keen to give it a go. He did say that if I needed his advice he would willingly help me, so I kept that in mind. He was then ninety-one years of age.

Eventually, when I had finished writing the script, I wanted his advice on the next move and tried to contact him but his health was failing fast and he was in a nursing home at Caton, near Lancaster. Olive, daughter Jean and I travelled by car to see him and took the script along with us. We found a big change in Mr Swale, as he was in bed and looked awful. He was still very pleased to see us and suggested we leave the script for him to go through and then he would eventually post it back to us with his recommendations. I was not to worry as it might take him a while.

Actually, it was not that long before the postman delivered the quite large package in a brown envelope to Guides Farm and I had a good idea of what was inside. Enclosed was a very scribbled letter from Eric, saying how much he had enjoyed reading through the script and that I was to break it up into chapters, giving each chapter a heading and then deciding on a title for the book. I also needed to put the whole script into chronological order and then either get in touch with our local newspaper to serialise it or better still find a publisher who would be willing to take it on.

I began to wonder how to proceed and a few days later, while leading a walk from Hest Bank to Grange, I came into conversation with a very well spoken man who was interested in my occupation as fisherman and Guide. He asked me many questions, but I could see that he was a well-educated person and very polite.

Everyone on the walk was enjoying themselves, meeting and making new friends on what was the most perfect day, with magnificent views whichever way you looked and so remarkably clear. We hadn't far to go before we arrived at the shore at Jenny Brown's Point and here we would all squat down on the rocky foreshore.

This point had taken us to the halfway stage of our journey and most of the walkers were ready for a break. Lots of them seemed to think it was picnic time and started opening their packs and got ready to enjoy whatever they had brought along with them. I like to find a secluded place away from the main party so I can reflect on the journey and what lies ahead. The gentleman whom I had met earlier came along and asked if I would mind if he sat down with me. I was glad he did, because I mentioned to him that I had written a script about my life and experiences on the sands and he said, "I think I can help you there." He took a pen and paper from his inside jacket pocket and wrote down the name of a publisher, David & Charles from Newton Abbot in Devon, whom he thought would be very interested in my kind of a book. He suggested that I write to them and explain its content, which I did and received a most favourable reply.

They asked me to send them some sample material. I posted three chapters to them and they liked what they saw and asked me to send the rest of the manuscript to them. It was immediately accepted and a contract was signed. We were all excited, here at the farm and our friends and neighbours from along Cart Lane, and now we were all anxious to see my book in print and on sale in the shops.

On publication in 1980, lots of signing sessions were organised for me to attend and the first was the station bookstall in Grange. I was sat there enjoying myself signing the new copies of *Sand Pilot of Morecambe Bay*, and things were going really well when a call came through from Granada Television at Manchester.

They wanted me to travel to their studios and said they would provide a taxi there and back. Times of arrival were given to me and I was told my interviewer would be Bob Smithies. I was so excited and could not wait to tell Olive, and she and the family were only too pleased for me to go. A taxi arrived and I was now about to be chauffeur driven to Manchester and back again.

Although I had not previously met Bob Smithies, I had seen him quite often on television but I still did not know what to expect. As we arrived and entered the building Bob met me with a strong handshake, but didn't waste much time in explaining the ropes. The temperature inside seemed to me unbearable, and I could feel my face getting redder and redder by the minute. He then led me to what he called the powder room and when he opened the door I could not help but notice well-known names such as Elsie Tanner and others written in chalk on all the mirrors above the dressing tables.

"Take a seat," Bob said, "Anywhere will do." I sat down in front of one of these large mirrors and Bob did the same but I think he had his own chair. I wondered whatever was going to happen next. We were soon both made up to appear before the television cameras, although I needed much more makeup than Bob. It seemed to me to be getting hotter by the minute and by this time you could have boiled a kettle on my head. I was powdered, had my eyebrows trimmed and sticking out bits lopped from my hair. I emerged looking and feeling like a circus clown.

All seemed to go to plan and I came home to a wonderful surprise party that Olive and family had organised for me. They had invited over good friends and neighbours so there was quite a house full. She had made a special cake in the shape of an open book with the title across the top icing. We all had more than a happy hour and a really great time with such a lovely buffet. It was a most memorable send-off for the new book.

When *Sand Pilot of Morecambe Bay* was re-published in 1998, Hannah Hauxwell wrote a new foreword. She had become a good friend as a result of her earlier visits to Abbot Hall at Kents Bank when on holiday, but now she stayed with us for a week and accompanied Olive and me to all the signing sessions, which she enjoyed. We also travelled to Radio Blackburn, with some good friends of ours, David and Anne Dewhurst. We called on them and Anne went along with us and showed us the way, which was most helpful as we were strangers to the town. Hannah and I broadcast live on the same subject. At the time there was a heavy snowfall and I was hoping and praying that it would not last. Luckily it disappeared almost as fast as it came down and we were able to travel all the way back to Grange in safety.

CHAPTER FIVE

Crossings to Remember

THE ROYAL CARRIAGE CROSSING

On the 30 May 1985, thousands witnessed the historic crossing of the Bay by the Duke of Edinburgh with his magnificent Cleveland Bays and eleven other carriages. The number was limited to twenty carriages for safety reasons but quite a number of entrants got cold feet at the last minute, having heard of the hidden dangers across Morecambe Bay. There had been times when I could have taken more horse-drawn carriages across the Bay without any problems, but on this occasion the Bay at the Silverdale side was the most difficult I had known it. To have taken twenty carriages across would have been very difficult and I was relieved when the final number of twelve was given to me.

This event needed some special thought and preparation. Yet only a matter of three weeks to the day of the crossing, conditions were still very uncertain. After all the weeks of planning, studying of the tides and tide tables, of weather forecasts and watching the movements of the Kent and gullies, to say nothing of the headaches as the river altered its course yet again, there was the added worry of continual rain. I could only wait and hope that things would improve.

In the meantime, enquiries were being made around the picturesque village of Silverdale for a suitable meeting place for the drivers and the vehicles carrying their horses and carriages. We needed to find somewhere with a good access for large vehicles and preferably as near to the shore as possible. After several visits to the area by me and later by Mr. Hugh Cavendish, now Lord Cavendish, and Mr Lee from Holker Hall, the ideal place was found on the outskirts of the village. Stone Bower Fellowship Home for the Elderly Disabled in Cove Road was a quiet, secluded place with a small meadow at the rear, but large enough for the needs of this occasion. The manager, Bernard Wood, was only too pleased to be involved and willingly gave permission.

Things were progressing slowly and the main worry was the weather. Tetley

Walker, the north-west brewery company, was sponsoring both the River Kent Crossing on May 30 and also the subsequent Holker Driving Trials and County Show. There had been press meetings at Holker Hall, but as yet nothing had been released to the public. There had been no official announcement that the Duke of Edinburgh would take part in the drive over the sands.

The police, the local chief coastguards, John Duerdon from Arnside, Don Shearer from Walney and myself were informed of progress at the meetings. A news information sheet had been compiled for the press by Brian Johnson, the Tetley Walker public relations officer in Manchester. Everything was in hand, waiting for confirmation from Buckingham Palace, and until this was forthcoming it had to be kept under wraps.

When it was officially announced that the Duke of Edinburgh was to take part in the drive over the sands, I was informed by Mrs Johnson of Holker Hall and the following day by BBC Television from Manchester.

A brief interview was needed for a news item, following which the press, the TV companies and the local radio stations were very, very, interested. From then on, our telephone was ringing incessantly, right up to the day of the drive. Many calls were from people enquiring where the drive was to start and how long it would take. Others wanted to know where I would be bringing them ashore. I had been warned by the police to contact them immediately if I had any suspect calls, but they all seemed genuine.

Before long I was to meet up with the organisers from Holker and representatives of Tetley Walker, including the driver of the two Shire horses, at the Kents Bank Hotel. This meeting was to put them in the picture a little bit more about the sands, the River Kent and the route I had in mind. After a drink and a bite to eat it was decided that we should make our way down to Kents Bank railway station and take a look at the railway crossing and walk down the causeway onto the sands. The day was fine, the tides low and the sands could not have looked better. Proposals were put forward and decisions taken and we all came away feeling that we had achieved something out of the meeting. Tetley Walker arranged to put their banners on the beach and the posts provided for them would also serve to keep the crowd under control.

I had some very good helpers to mark out the route from the Silverdale side and it took us two days, using two hundred 'brobs' from rhododendron bushes to a point almost half way across the Bay. The route was not straight across, but snaked to and fro to avoid large areas of shifting sands. This also added to the distance, which was approximately six miles.

No more could be done at this stage from the Silverdale side as it was now Wednesday evening and we had yet to travel back to Grange. The rest of the route out from Kents Bank was much safer but still had to be marked for the drivers to follow, without me forever giving them instructions on where to go.

On the night of May 29 I went to sleep knowing that I had done everything humanly possible to make the crossing for his Royal Highness and friends pleasurable and, above all, safe.

I thought it would be to our advantage to make an early start on the morning of May 30 along with my helpers. We set out from the farm at 3.30am following the safest route, which still needed some markers to be put in the sand. When we arrived at the Kent for the final check, before the drive on the sands in the afternoon following the next tide, you would have never believed that a river could behave in such a way. It had moved at least 150 yards away from the markers put in the sand only the day before. After testing the bed of the new river for firmness, it had improved itself and I was more satisfied than I had ever been before. We just had to move a few of the original markers and replace those that had been washed away. We turned for home as dawn broke with a clear sky and, as we watched the sun rise, we knew then that we were in for a perfect day.

The drive was to leave the far side of the Bay from Stone Bower at 3.30pm. Meanwhile back at Guides Farm, all was bustling with activity. Olive and daughter Jean were baking and preparing lots of nice things as they had decided to lay on a buffet for our helpers and friends when we all met back home after the crossing.

We had all heard the terrifying stories of the lives the Bay had claimed, as locals were taught a deep respect for the dangers behind its natural beauty, but they all seemed very remote on that hot and glorious day. The world's press were there, just in case the trip to mark the tenth anniversary of the Holker Driving Trials misfired. I overheard someone ask Prince Philip why he was making the crossing and was he not just a little bit apprehensive.

He replied, "No, of course I am not apprehensive. I would not be doing this if I thought there would be any risk at all." The Duke's poor regard for pressmen is well known and his lack of patience was obvious, but in the meadow behind Stone Bower he seemed relaxed and cheerful as the grooms made finishing touches to the team of magnificent Cleveland Bays. The Duke was asked if he had ever driven on the sands before with a carriage and team. "No," he replied, "Nor has anyone else here attempted the sands before." He added that he never got the opportunity to cross sands as there were none at Windsor Castle or Sandringham!

At this point he did admit that there was a slight risk, but no, he was not anxious: "I have every confidence in my guide." He now stepped down from the gleaming black and gold marathon carriage to join me for the drivers' briefing. As they gathered around me to listen to what I had to say, I explained that the drive was not dangerous, providing they observed and stuck to what I told them:

Transport for the Press corps during the royal carriage crossing on 30 May 1985. The Dike of Edinburgh displayed his customary lack of patience with the pressmen. (Peter Cherry)

"We are going out there to have a jolly good day out and we will enjoy it. It is something different and certainly will be a great experience."

"Let's see if it's a great experience at the end of the trip," the Duke remarked.

Minutes after leaving Stone Bower and driving down Cove Lane, we approached the marshes. The Duke, leading the procession, lost sight of the route markers in the milling crowd and took a wrong turn and I had to put him right. He showed visible annoyance at the noise from the helicopters overhead and spectators running in the path of the horses as I tried to line them up. There were many different carriages and teams of horses – some single, others tandem, and the four in hands. I did not want them all of a heap, following each other, as that would soften up the sand and make it more dangerous. It was hard at this point because the public would not keep at bay. One dear old lady came up and got hold of the bridle of one of the Duke's leading horses and started to stroke him.

There was only one policeman on hand at this stage and things were getting a bit out of hand. I suddenly thought, right, I'll blow my whistle and all of a

The awe-inspiring sight of the Duke of Edinburgh's carriage-and-four with its magnificent Cleveland horses. The Duke was in no mood to take the crossing at a leisurely canter and I had to keep telling him to slow down his team. (Peter Cherry)

sudden the public opened up a wide expanse so that we could now see where we were going and we were off. Prince Philip's carriage moved off at a great rate towards the river and I had in my mind what the organisers of the Drive had told me previously: "Do not let the Duke have his own way." The time had been estimated for the crossing and, although I constantly asked the Duke to slow down his team as we were leaving all the others behind, he wanted to know why he should do so. I had to tell him!

It was only now that the other drivers could relax and take in the sweeping panorama of the Bay. The actual crossing of the River Kent shortly after negotiating the softer sands on the Silverdale side was a very pleasant experience.

The Duke's verdict on the crossing was that it had been delightful, apart from the noise from the helicopters. He also said that his team of horses needed a little of their strength sapping for the driving trials and crossing was the ideal exercise to calm them down. By now, lots of people had walked out to meet us and were running alongside with their cameras and taking shots of the Duke. At one stage a young boy on his bicycle rode straight into the path of Prince Philip's horses.

I was at last able to relax when we reached Kents Bank and were surrounded by large crowds. It was a fitting end to the most memorable day of my life. (Peter Cherry)

Sweeping this minor annoyance aside the Duke seemed in high spirits.

As we now approached the large crowds towards the end of this historic crossing, cheers went up and HRH spoke to me saying, "Stand up, Mr Robinson, it's you they are cheering, not me!" I didn't, though the atmosphere, with everyone looking so happy and in carnival mood with the brass band playing as the royal carriage pulled up at Kents Bank, gave me this unbelievable feeling. It really filled me up inside. We had conquered the Bay with its unpredictable moods and tides and quicksand.

This was certainly the most memorable day of my life. It was now time for the local dignitaries to meet the Duke, followed by a presentation by Tetley Walker Limited of an inscribed glass tankard to commemorate the Kent Sands crossing by horse-drawn carriages. As the Duke was presented with the tankard, he immediately asked if there was one for me. As there was only one, he gave it to me. I was surprised but also very pleased and thanked him very much.

The time had now come to move off the sands with the horses, over the newly laid boards, over the railway crossing and onto the road and under the shade of some trees near to Priory Lane. I now climbed down from the royal carriage, my assignment being completed and made my way up to Kents Bank Hotel to meet up with my friends. It was question time for the press and then it was time for me to go home to Olive and our family and friends and have our own little celebration. To add to the appreciation of the successful sands crossing, one week later I received a letter of warm thanks from Lady Cavendish saying it had been a wonderful success and a magical experience. On June 13, Olive and I were invited to have lunch at Holker Hall with the Cavendish family and Mr Lea, which we were very pleased to accept and greatly enjoyed. Another nice surprise for us the following day was to receive a kind letter of thanks from Buckingham Palace.

HORSES AND RIDERS

Ribble Valley Driving Club has been coming up into this area now for a number of years. They are given permission to stay on Cartmel Park adjacent to the racecourse, where there is ample room to park up with their horseboxes and caravans and lots of lush grass where they can tether up their horses. This is one of the Club's favourite outings and whilst they are up in the area for a week, I organise a carriage crossing for them if the weather and tide permit. They always drive their horses and ponies down to Kents Bank railway station and then comes the most exciting part of crossing the sands over to Arnside in the area of White Creek. After giving their horses and ponies a rest, we return by the way we came out, crossing the Kent on both journeys. The sands and river crossing have to be tested the day previously and weather conditions taken into account.

These horses are exceptionally fit as they do a lot of roadwork prior to coming to Cartmel. All of them enjoy the river crossing and most times on the return journey the drivers get them going full trot, or even at a gallop. You can imagine water splashing everywhere, with us coming out of the river on the Grange side and all of us dripping wet. But we have all enjoyed the ride across the Bay and so have the horses. We seem to dry out in no time at all, with the warm breeze and the sunshine. Back at the shore, all that now remains is for the horses and carriages to cross safely over the railway and then they have the long drive back to Cartmel.

I see them off at a trot up the steep hill towards Allithwaite and, as I get into my car, all as I can hear in the distance is the clatter of the metal horseshoes on the hard surface of tarmacadam roads. When they arrive back at their base and unyoke and tether their horses, they will no doubt do some reminiscing about the crossing of the perilous but beautiful Morecambe Bay and go home thinking about another crossing of the sands next year.

With the ever-increasing traffic and congested roads, is there any wonder that crossing the Bay with horses – both riders and horse-drawn carriages – has become an annual event?

Phyllis, from Hellifield, a mad keen and very experienced horsewoman, has been organising these events for a number of years. When she first rang and told me of the number of riders she would like to bring along, I had to suggest that I would rather lead the way across the sands from a horse-drawn carriage, as I had not ridden a horse for years and that I did not fancy falling off in the middle of the River Kent. She laughed but was most helpful and said she knew of a friend who lived at Rathmell, near Settle, who had a turnout that she thought would be suitable to do the job. Brian Proctor agreed and arrived with his horse and carriage, which immediately took my eye. It was a fine looking grey gelding with a suitable name – 'Spirit'!

On our very first trip across the Bay, with Craven Bridle Club, the Lancashire Group and others from the Furness area, there was fun and games at the start. I phoned the signalman from Kents Bank railway station to confirm it was safe to cross. Railway lines are something different to what these horses had ever encountered. Most of them hesitated and had to be led in order to give them confidence. The next obstacles were way ahead at the few water-filled dykes and gullies, which start way out at the far end of the marsh. Again, fun and games, but the experienced riders took a grip of their mounts and, with a little patience, cleared the dykes and gullies. Some of the horses took an almighty leap, but once clear of the shore, everyone seemed more at ease. As we arrived at the Kent, I stepped down from my carriage to have a word with the riders, asking them to spread out and keep that way through the river.

I had been out the day before with my helpers and we had crossed the river with my tractor and marked out the route the whole of the way with laurel bushes. I did ask the riders to let us go on ahead in the carriage before they came through at a gallop.

The Kent was about three feet deep with quite a flow. Markers had been put in the sand at either side of the river to show the safe width. When it was time to move out I explained to Brian to make for the top marker, on the left, but as we got deeper, and a faster flow, Brian was making downstream instead of across, so I grabbed the reins and said "What are you doing? I did say to you to make for the top marker and keep going in that direction."

Brian replied, "We're floating."

Although this was not the case, as a stranger both to the sands and crossing a moving river, Brian was convinced that we were afloat. I explained to him, "Never, ever look down when you are going through a fast moving river, as it has this effect on you. Best set your eyes on the far side and keep looking that way until you have reached the other side."

My father used to tell me the same thing and the problems he had with horses new to the sands when crossing the river, "You had an 'eck of a job to drive them straight across from one side to the other."

Brian has now been on several trips across the Bay and got used to the crossing of the river.

Following this ride, I had a request from Phyllis's husband, who had been on all the drives and rides across the Bay. He had ridden on my 'Sandpiper' trailer with his son, who on two occasions took shots that he made into a video and DVD. He told me that he had a horse and carriage but did not like bringing it as his horse just did not go so well with others around. I agreed with him and found a date later on in the year. In the meantime, Brian rang to tell me that he had bought a Friesian stallion with a good temperament. He and Phyllis had broken it into harness and would it be alright if he brought it along on the trip I had already organised with her husband. My answer was yes and I said I would ride alongside Phyllis's husband with his horse up front.

On the day they arrived at Kents Bank station for the ride across the sands to Arnside and back, there were three horse-drawn vehicles and three outriders. Phyllis's husband yoked up his dun coloured horse and it seemed very quiet. Brian needed a bit of help putting his stallion between the shafts and when he did get it yoked, it would not stand, so he kept it moving by going round and round in huge circles on the road just outside the railway station. It was such a good-looking animal with a nice head carriage. One other Friesian mare, a much bigger horse than Brian's in every way but still an eye catcher, was to go on the drive. Apart from Phyllis with her Spanish flying machine, there were also two more riders on thoroughbreds.

The day went well and I could not take my eye off Brian's stallion. It went so well at the walk and the trot, with its head held high and it moved along like a hackney. It took to the river straight away and the journey across the Bay seemed nothing to it. On returning they thanked me, as always, and then gave their horses a feed before making the journey back to Yorkshire. Sometime later I received through the post a DVD of that crossing of the sands, which we have watched in the comfort of our armchairs at Guides Farm. We cannot wait until the next season comes around when we can do this all over again.

The geese get ready for the 'off' and prepare to head across Morecambe Bay on their epic journey from Furness Abbey to Whitby.

A GAGGLE OF GEESE

In July 2000 I had a very unusual request from a young woman from Whitby, who wanted to raise money for a twelve-year old arthritis sufferer. She planned to walk with seventeen geese, starting on the west coast at Furness Abbey, and then crossing the Bay from Kents Bank to Arnside before finishing their long trek across the country at Whitby on the east coast. I agreed to lead them across the Bay and arrangements and times were given to the organisers for me to meet up with them and their geese on the edge of the grass out from Kents Bank railway station. I suggested that if they could make it to arrive at Kents Bank shore the night before the crossing of the sands, the geese would have a well-earned rest before tackling the sands and river crossing the following day.

This was agreed by the organisers. All that I needed to know from them when I arrived down at the shore the next day was how fast does a goose walk. We would not want to arrive at the river too early or it would be too deep for me to cross. Lucy Muller said that her geese were very tired from the previous day's walk so she thought that they would only go at a slow pace. I had visions of them taking flight when we got out into the wide open space of the Bay, but they could not have behaved in a better way. After a few photo shots by local people who had turned up to watch this extraordinary event, a TV team arrived just in time for a brief interview with me before we started our trek across the marsh and over the Bay to Arnside.

I was accompanied by my granddaughters, Amy Robinson and Danielle Nickson, and we set off at quite a pace as the geese following us were hard on our heels. Once out onto the sand, I tested them by meandering first to the left and then to the right, and they followed my every move. There would have been no need for the driver Lucy Muller and her collie dog, as they behaved so well, and they must have thought I was Mother Goose! We arrived at the River Kent and crossed in style, with all the geese paddling like mad to keep with me and not to be taken downstream. I was amazed!

We then made over on higher ground towards White Creek, Arnside, which I believed was going to be their overnight stop. Lucy Muller achieved her goal and I think the highlight of their long journey would definitely have been the crossing of Morecambe Bay.

LAND ROVERS ACROSS THE BAY

It is a challenge of a lifetime to drive across the Bay and back again without getting stuck. Thousands of people have walked across under my guidance but the very first enquiry for taking four 4x4 vehicles came about fifteen years ago. It followed a much publicised reclassification of a path across the Bay to a 'Byway open to all vehicular traffic' in accordance with the Wildlife and Countryside Act 1981. This gave people the wrong impression and I am telling you now that there is nothing so queer as folk, as long as they are alive!

I was receiving calls almost every minute of the day – stupid calls with the general public thinking there was now a tarmacadam road all the way across the Bay. I had a lot of explaining to do, with most of the enquirers giving up on the idea. There is just no route or pathway across Morecambe Bay safe for the general public, unless they are accompanied by a 'Sand Grown' person or the official guide, who has the experience of living the sands with all their moods. Timings of high tides and knowledge of incoming tides are critical. The route varies from one day to the next due to tides and storms, and avoiding quicksand and deeper channels is essential.

The route on the enclosure map is currently impossible due to vast changes

Winter morning at Arnside, looking across the ever-changing sands of Morecambe Bay towards Grange. (Peter Cherry)

in the Kent and Keer channels. The only vehicular access onto the Bay from the other side was from Bolton-le-Sands, which is much further up the coast than Hest Bank on the Morecambe Lodge Farm area. Safety at all times is my concern, so the sands and the river crossing have to be tested the day before any event can take place I can read the sands from my tractor as I drive along, but there is one thing I cannot do, and that is to know what lies under the water in the River Kent Crossing. I always have my helpers with me to test the bed of the river; we are invariably barefooted and carry a long ash stick to prod for quicksand. When I am perfectly satisfied, my friends wade through the river to the far side. I turn around and wade back towards my tractor, then cross the river and pick them up and continue across the sands to the White Creek area of Arnside.

We always take with us a flask and biscuits and stop the tractor close to the shore. Here we jump off and enjoy a short break before returning the same way we came, putting out our laurel markers in readiness to follow the same route the next day. Usually on the return journey the River Kent will have ebbed and is much shallower than when we crossed it earlier. It is essential here to mark out the safe width with the laurels, so that on the drive the next day there will be ample room for the drivers to spread out and not follow in each other's tracks.

A typical expedition took us across sixteen miles of sand, deep gullies and the River Kent crossing. As we set off from Kents Bank the views across the Bay and towards Arnside slowly began to become clearer as we followed the markers put in the day before. The start of the drive took us over the wet and very slippery marshland, then down a seven-foot gully and into deep dykes running towards the River Kent. Once, when we had crossed the river, I was asked if our return journey would be on the same route. Some of the drivers had the horrible feeling that their vehicles were going to stall in the fast flowing river. The Kent was about 200 yards wide, but once the vehicles hit the river the drivers soon felt the pull of the ebbing tide and had to hold really firm to the steering wheel.

I always ask people to fix their eyes on a point on the headland and not to deviate from it when crossing the river, as it is so easy to be pulled off line and into danger. It was a tough struggle to keep the vehicles on an even keel, and one of the drivers thought that we were floating. I assured him that we weren't and that it was the feeling everyone got when crossing a fast moving river for the first time.

It was now time to press on for the shore at White Creek at Arnside, which gave the drivers a strange sensation in going over wet shimmering sands. After a while we came up onto much higher ground, where the tide had not reached and the sand had dried out. We drove close to the rocks and stopped, but hardly long enough for a tea break as they wanted a photo shoot. We then made our way back across the sands the way we came and once again tackled the river crossing.

The afternoon sunlight was bouncing off the wet sands and the river in the distance. Now we had to cross the river once again, but this way there were no easy landmarks on which the drivers could focus. However, they managed to cross safely and head back towards Kents Bank. It had taken us around four hours back to the slipway and the railway crossing, and the drive across the sands had been a truly amazing experience.

CHAPTER SIX

Celebrated Occasions

MY VERY FIRST INTERVIEW after settling into our new home was by Alistair McDonald and Stuart Hall, in the spring of 1964 for BBC Radio. It was thought that the most suitable place was on the shore, in a secluded spot, down from the Cart Lane railway crossing. We had to find some bushes where we could be hidden from the wary eyes of the birds and they set up their equipment to do the recording. All seemed to go well as I talked about the cross-Bay walks with the sound of the sea birds being picked up in the distance. But we had to stop recording when the trains went past and start all over again.

On the night the programme was to be broadcast, the whole family and several friends came along to listen and there were so many of us that we had to sit two to a chair, and some even sat on the living room floor. You could have heard a pin drop. Then when the programme was announced, followed by my broadcast, it seemed to be over in such a short time, but everyone thought it most interesting.

Following this, I gave another interview with Bob Langley for BBC Radio for the programme 'Pebble Mill at One'. There was now a certain added interest from many journalists, reporters and writers, both locally and far afield.

In February 1967 I was involved with a film for BBC television 'Look North' and at the end of July 1974 was to take part in a series called 'Lakeland Summer'. I was on horseback as in the old days, leading a pair of horses over the sands in my role as Guide. This programme was repeated on BBC2 the following April.

On 9 September 1974, I received a letter with a request for my services as Guide to accompany a man and his Chinese wheelbarrow on a desert cart across the Bay from one side to the other. This would be a distance of eight to ten miles. A further letter came with all the details of the desert cart. It was a lightweight construction with a wheel five-foot in diameter and long, narrow boxes, one on either side of the wheel to carry the load. The disposal of the load in this way put the weight on the cart, not on the driver. A sail was used to take advantage of any favourable wind, leaving only the guiding of the cart to the driver, and enabling him to cover many more miles than would have been the case had he needed to push or pull the load in the normal way.

The whole idea was to test the cart out in the stringent conditions of the Bay before taking it out to the Sahara Desert for a further test, after which it was hoped to put it into production. It would have been of great use to the people in this kind of area, who could not afford to use motorised transport or camels to move their wares. The vehicle was to be manufactured by a well-known British firm, and the Morecambe Bay test was covered by a BBC 'Nationwide' helicopter.

Crossing the Bay went fairly well, but it was apparently a different matter when the cart reached the Sahara. The wind strength there was much greater and the wheels were found to be too narrow. All in all, the going was very hard. Eventually it was decided not to put the cart into production but the prototype is preserved in store at the Science Museum, South Kensington. This was one of the most unusual trips I made across the Bay.

In the last week of October 1975 I was approached by Granada television to make a thirty-minute film, which they called 'Sand Pilot'. I invited two fishing pals, Brian Shaw and Harold Benson from Flookburgh, along to Guides Farm. All three of us were involved in the making of the film and it turned out to be a winner.

'Blue Peter' was always a popular programme and it was such a pleasure to meet up with the film crew. Simon Groom was the interviewer as we filmed way out in the Bay, and there was also Goldie, their retriever, who enjoyed splashing about in the watery dykes and gullies.

I must say that I really enjoyed taking part in the TV programme 'Treasure Hunt'. George Bowman, from Penrith, came along with his wonderful horses and carriages, especially for the programme. These were our transport across the Bay to the area marked out where the helicopter would eventually find us – and the clue – in the sands. It seemed an age before we spotted the helicopter, and I think we saw it long before they could see us, but it was exciting and made a very good programme.

QUICKSAND

I shall always remember Professor Magnus Pike's programme, when someone asked the question, "What makes quicksand?" Lots of time went into the filming in a really dangerous area, but it was just right for the programme, which was an almighty success. We didn't lose anyone! We only lost half a dummy, which was used as a last resort.

Earlier, the co-pilot from a stand-by air-sea rescue helicopter had the frightening experience of getting stuck up to his knees in the quicksand and the helicopter had a difficult time trying hard to lift him free. He was not up for this a second time around so the film company made this huge dummy. It was at least eight feet tall and, because of its size and weight, it was hoped that it would sink down in the quicksand. It did but only to about waist deep.

The helicopter came over and let down a rope like a noose, which fell nicely into place. Now all they had to do was to rev the engines on full power and hope the dummy, fast in the quicksand, would free itself when they operated the winch. It wouldn't move! At first it seemed that the helicopter was coming down, but no matter how much they tried, they had to leave the dummy stuck in the quicksand.

It was there for some weeks, and people kept ringing Guides Farm to say that there was a man drowning in the Bay. Some days there was nothing to be seen and other times, when the tide had scoured around it, the dummy was more visible. One day it was in shallow water and I seized my opportunity.

Olive has a saying, "When the tide goes out, so does Cedric!" It was now time to stop the incessant phone calls, so I went over to my shed in the yard and got my bushman saw. Telling Olive that I wouldn't be too long, I crossed the Cart Lane railway crossing and walked the short distance to the dummy. I was now going to get wet and muddy as I lay down, spreading my weight so as not to join him. I gritted my teeth and sawed him off at his waist, almost level with the sands. The tides were running high and I just had the time to walk back to the farm, get a change of clothing and look out of the bedroom window.

As the tidal bore reached the dummy, it picked up the top half and carried it towards the Grange over Sands promenade. I thought, "Now, what have I done." I had stopped the phone calls about the man drowning in the Bay, but now I was thinking of some dear old lady walking her dog on the promenade and getting the shock of her life, seeing half a body being brought in with the tide. I feared the phone calls would start up once again!

Quicksand was also to the fore when an American film company rang me to ask if it would be possible for them to come over to England. They had read an account in *Readers Digest* that a person had been trapped up to his waist in Morecambe Bay. His cries for help were not heard because the wind direction was taking them out to sea. He was stuck fast in the sand all night. Luckily for him the tides were low, but were to rise the next morning with the wind changing to the west. His cries were then heard and he was saved – only at the very last minute – as the tide lapped him and his rescuers.

A date was fixed for the Americans to arrive at Kents Bank. I had been out on the sands previously to the River Kent and found some dangerous but exciting

A dramatic 'brack' – a breakaway of sand – near Silverdale. Such features are often associated with quicksand, as I was able to show an American film company in search of danger. (Peter Cherry)

areas of quicksand. Olive always keeps an eye on me when I am out there alone, and especially on this occasion when the quicksand was right on the edge of the river and low down, so that sometimes I would be out of sight from the shore. The day the Americans chose for filming was one when I had already booked a small school party, but they said they did not mind as they could involve them in the programme.

On the day I met up with the film crew at Kents Bank railway station and was introduced to the children and their teacher. Then we were off over the marsh and onto the sand. Before we had gone very far, the producer came to me and said, "Mr Robinson, we have just been thinking, is it not too dangerous to go out all that way, can't we find some quicksand a little bit milder, nearer the shore?"

"Yes I can," was my answer, but after them coming specially all that way, I thought, "Right, I must quickly find them the most dangerous sands as now they are losing their nerve." This was not a problem as way over to the right of where we were walking was a very deep gulley, which runs out from the land. I noticed a huge 'brack' (a breakaway of sand) and decided this was the right place. As we approached, I blew my whistle to hold everyone and went on ahead to test the sands in this deep gulley. The producer was by my side and was pleased with what he saw as I tested with my stick – the area was quite frightening.

I now called and beckoned the party, film crew and the children towards me, marking a distinctive line across the sands with my stick as a safe area from which to watch and not to cross whatsoever. The camera was set up and now it was time for me to demonstrate. All went well and the producer suggested I took one of the children along with me. When we asked for a volunteer, all of them wanted to go down in the quicksand. I could only manage one for safety reasons but that very young child had an unforgettable experience and the crew put together a very good film. They did eventually send me a tape and all of the children on the day had the time of their lives

MELVYN BRAGG

The list of distinguished visitors to Guides Farm in the past seems endless – some to take part in films out in the Bay, and others to participate in the famous cross-Bay walk.

I took Melvyn Bragg (now Lord Bragg) across the Bay from Hest Bank to Kents Bank on a glorious day. The reason Melvyn wished to accompany me on a walk was to get the sensation of being out on the Bay, which he wanted to convey in a book he was about to write, entitled *The Maid of Buttermere*. He could not have come on a more ideal day and I did enjoy his company.

Melvyn later wrote an article in *Punch* about his experience of crossing the sands, from which the following extract is taken:

"There are people you meet who come straight out of a book, even in our sophisticated times when such a nice and simple phrase might seem rarer than a Nigerian Turnip, even in our television age (when actually more books are read, but let that pass) when we are collectively accused of reneging on the fine print. Even so, these people do exist, only sometimes as 'characters' and they can step out of the pages and into your life without so much as a (book) token of acknowledgement of the difference between life and fiction. I met a man the other day. He led me across the sands of Morecambe Bay. Cedric Robinson is the Queen's Guide to the Sands, but also takes the title of Sand Pilot. It is a title which evokes the ancient and the romantic.

"Pilot has been an inspiration, a metaphor, a hope. Tennyson – 'I hope to see my pilot face to face when I have crossed the bar' and those who bear that title inherit the ancient Kingdom of Trust. You feel some of that as you trudge out across the Morecambe Bay Sands.

"When Wordsworth resettled in the Lakes on Christmas Eve, 1799, it was a place in which those binding nourishing rural communities and those open plain but heroic people who are the most cherished characters and in his work could still be found. For Wordsworth they had links with Arcadia, and with the deep decency of an honest endeavour which encountered the largest claims with stoicism and drear sustenance, even Solace from nature. 'Michael' is the most vivid of these creations – a shepherd whose only son abandoned him for the corrupting city and left him without an heir, without hope, stricken down but always a man of worth.

"I suspect that Cedric Robinson would find such an introduction and such a comparison embarrassing, but it is there. If you know the Lakes and knew Wordsworth, then you have met him before and he does not let you down.

"Even his turn of phrase reaches back, 'And it was done – And so we did' – while his appearance, strong, thatched grey hair, cheeks apple ripe with the weather, movement at once steady and alert, come straight from resolution and independence."

BILL BRYSON

When I heard that Bill Bryson was making a documentary on Morecambe Bay, I was asked to gather a group of people together who would be available and interested in taking part. The first person that I approached was a really nice man – a gentleman whom I had no more than passed the time of day with at our garden gate. When I knew the date that the filming was to take place, he said he was definitely interested. He and his wife had heard so much of the cross-Bay walks, and so now he was looking forward to the filming in the Bay and meeting up with the well- known Bill Bryson. On the day, the weather was quite cool with it being out of season and the producer of the documentary said to me that he would prefer just a small group to take part out in the Bay.

I didn't have any problems with that as I had a few contacts I could ring. The manageress at Abbot Hall Methodist Holiday Home was pleased that I phoned her and the numbers of walkers were then made up with the addition of one or two locals.

The plan was for me to meet up with them on the foreshore out from Kents Bank railway station and to bring along my tractor pulling the Sandpiper. Although the day seemed nice enough and clear as a bell, there was quite a cold wind, so everyone was asked to wrap up well for this walk, as once out in the Bay there is no shelter from the shore.

On meeting Bill Bryson, you quickly feel that you have known him all your life. He was soon to tell me that he never felt entirely comfortable with British seaside weather, even on the sunniest days in summer, but although he grew up almost a thousand miles from the sea, the reason he liked Morecambe Bay so much was that it was compact and pretty. Much of the time there was not much water in it at all, and that was his kind of bay. Bill had a conversation with one of the group whom I mentioned above. He was wearing a pair of low cut shoes with socks and carrying a thumb stick. He really enjoyed talking to Bill, as he had been on the sands with me before on one of my walks and never forgot the lovely experience.

He described the sands and the river crossing so well that you would have thought he had known them all his life. "There is always one," he commented. "They are there to tell you that what you are about to do is not as you imagined."

Before setting out across the Bay, Bill was given my book *Sand Pilot of Morecambe Bay*. Some words in it put doubt in his mind as he read, "Across the sands of Morecambe Bay the tide advances faster than a man can run, quicksands and ever changing channels have in the past claimed countless lives. And now it is not uncommon for holidaymakers to find themselves in difficulty."

The doubt changed when I spoke to the group and this seemed to give him more confidence. As we walked, we chatted and stopped occasionally to be filmed. Bill thought it odd to reflect that only a few hours earlier the spot where we were now walking had been under at least twenty feet of water. We were now fast approaching the River Kent crossing, and from where we were it looked positively enormous and very, very wide. I jokingly shouted ahead of the group, "Any non-swimmers?"

The tractor and Sandpiper were alongside us just in case. Bill had very few rules in life, so he said, but one of them was never to wade across a body of water when you could not see to the other side. Another was never to immerse yourself in anything colder than liquid nitrogen!

As we made our way into the river, I could not stop myself from laughing as I saw the look on most of the group's faces. Bill immediately said that he could feel his bones cracking and the odd pained numbness with the sensation that his toes were about to fall off. Someone in the group spoke and Bill said, "He didn't really say that this was lovely – did he?"

When we eventually did arrive safely at the other side, Bill took the shoulder of someone so as to not lose his balance, emptied out the water from his wellies and then put them back on again. The last leg of our journey was now in sight as we headed along the shore for White Creek, which took us about twenty minutes. Now on high ground we looked back over the way we had come and it was so clear that the views in every direction were really outstanding. Crossing the River Kent was now the sole topic of conversation. Although most of the group were feeling the cold, every one of us had a good laugh when Bill told us that the producer was probably sitting quite comfortably in a warm pub somewhere in Arnside waiting for us.

ALAN TITCHMARSH

In May 2003 I had the pleasure of meeting Alan Titchmarsh and being filmed out in the Bay with him. I took my Sandpiper tractor and trailer along to accommodate the film crew and all their equipment. My good friend Roger Arnold, sales manager of Great Northern Books, was on holiday and was very pleased when I asked him if he would like to come along with us out into the Bay and watch the filming. I was glad he agreed because when the crew finished their work the shots were now going to be taken from the air from a helicopter, and they did not want anyone else to be out there on the sands at that time.

Roger kindly offered to drive the tractor and Sandpiper back to the shore. He had never driven a tractor before, but did manage with no major difficulties except through the last deep dyke. Here he let the clutch out too quickly and threw all of the crew to the back of the Sandpiper!

Now there was just the two of us out there, Alan and I waiting for the helicopter and walking towards the open sea. I remarked to Alan that if we did not see the helicopter before long, we were really going to get our feet wet. Suddenly as if out of nowhere, this huge bird in the sky came nearer and got louder and much, much bigger. They had arrived and flew over us with several

takes. You are always told before being filmed, never to look at the camera, so we kept our eyes fixed straight ahead and hoped for the best. It is a most frightening experience with a helicopter coming towards you at speed, flying as low as is permitted. We both had haircuts out there that day, and some would describe the filming from above as 'a close shave.'

The helicopter left as fast as it came and only the two of us were out there miles from anywhere with no transport home. Then after a while my tractor and Sandpiper came into view with Roger behind the wheel. He told us of his earlier journey back to the shore and now suggested that I drove back to land. This I did and we all met up back on the shore at Kents Bank, with Roger taking several shots of us with my new camera. One very good one is used on the facing page. . The day was perfect for us and we could not have enjoyed ourselves more.

RICK STEIN

The very well-known seafood chef seemed delighted when he was to be filmed out in the Bay at the cockle beds and the fluke nets. When he was being interviewed on film, he kept forgetting his lines and looking on at a distance. I could not help laughing to myself. Not aloud, as all has to be kept quiet when the camera is running. He must have had about six takes. "Cut – can we have that again please?" was all I heard.

Eventually it was my turn. The interviewer always has on paper the question they are about to ask you. Usually things are straight forward but not always. I was interviewed at length on camera, but then they would stop, look at what they had just taken and say to me, "Sorry about this Cedric, but can we have that interview again?"

I always agreed, but would tell them that it would not be quite the same, as I did not have a script and just said what came into my head at the time. They were always agreeable to that and the interviews ran smoothly.

Rick came back to Guides Farm and cooked flounder fillets, shallow fried in breadcrumbs, then put them on a metal rack to drain. Now came his speciality – Hollandaise sauce, which he made with our freshly laid hen eggs. This was poured over the fillets and very much enjoyed. Rick said that flounder fillets done in this way were much tastier than halibut. Olive and I agreed with him and use this recipe regularly during the season.

Relaxing with Alan Titchmarsh after a wonderful day filming out in the Bay. It involved much helicopter work and several scary moments. (Roger Arnold)

DAVID BELLAMY

It was arranged that David Bellamy would arrive at Kents Bank by train, and that I would already be on the sands on my tractor with a small group of children from Barrow in Furness and the film crew.

As soon as we heard the train stop and then pull out of the station, the producer told me to start out into the Bay, which was knee deep in mud. David was running to catch up with us and shouting, "Wait for me! Wait for me!" Eventually we did stop and he clambered aboard. The children made a really good start to the day, with laughing at David struggling through the mud.

When we arrived at our destination for the filming, everyone jumped from the tractor. The children started stamping up and down on the sands and beginning to find young cockles, small and various colours of bivalves (named 'hen-pennies' by the local fishermen), and lots of very young shrimps. I remember David asking my grandson, Daniel, who was five years old at the time, if he would like to be the Guide over the Sands like his granddad when he grew up. He replied, "I fink so." He is now a fine looking young man aged twenty-nine.

The programme came over well on television and at a later date we here at Guides Farm received a high-quality videocassette from the TV company.

MORE CELEBRITIES

I have taken many other famous people across the sands. Here are all but a few of them:

Matthew Kelly participated in a school trip out into the Bay on my tractor and trailer. Matthew kept the children amused as we showed them the quicksand. When we returned after what had been such an exciting time for the children, they were met by their parents at Kents Bank railway station. Matthew and his film crew, along with Olive and I, were invited to tea at Abbot Hall Methodist Guild Holiday Home.

Olive and I with David Bellamy. His visit included some memorable antics out in the Bay with local children. (F W J Broomfield)

Judith Chalmers: The 'Wish you were Here' holiday programme was being filmed in Morecambe and, when Judith heard about the walks across the Bay, she and the film crew could not get over to Grange over Sands quick enough. Judith asked to use our bathroom and when she emerged we could not but notice how tanned she looked. This changed dramatically after spending time in the River Kent. The water washed the colour from her legs, but this gave us all a laugh out there and many happy memories.

Victoria Wood took part in a cross-Bay walk. I was told previously that she would be coming but to keep it low key. When she arrived at Arnside, we were introduced to each other. No one would have recognised her on this occasion as she wore a hat with a large peak low down so as not to disclose her face. After the walk, she and her minder thanked me, but among all those walkers on the day she was not recognised and this pleased her.

Harry Secombe: The late Sir Harry Secombe was probably one of the jolliest people one could ever wish to have met. I had this opportunity and it was a most wonderful experience, to be filmed for the Sunday Programme 'Highway.' Once again we met at Kents Bank railway station, where the filming started with Harry singing 'Show me the way.'

Hayley from 'Coronation Street' crossed the sands on an organised walk to raise money for the Parkinson's Disease charity. A most horrible walk weather wise, it rained from start to finish but this did not dampen Hayley's spirits. She is a lovely warm person, who at the end of the walk signed autographs for everyone who asked her to do so.

Fred Talbot: Fred has visited us here at the farm on two occasions. He came along in his little red bubble car and just loved the place. Also he said that he would like one day to come again and spend more time and join in one of my walks.

Neil Oliver: The programme 'Coast' has been repeated many times on television. It was a pleasure being filmed and then interviewed by the popular Neil.

Ian McKellen, the well-known actor, screen and television personality, was filmed out in the Bay. My role was to take the filming party out to the location I had chosen, then stand well back, keep quiet and watch. All went well on such a lovely day.

The Houghton Weavers after I had taken them across the Bay in July 2008 to raise money for a local charity. On my left are Tony Berry and Steve Millington, and on my right is David Littler. (John Thompson)

The Houghton Weavers crossed the Bay under my guidance in July 2008 to raise money for a charity of their choice. Following the event, Olive and I attended their show at Morecambe in March 2009 as guests. It was a sell-out and was fantastic!

'Flog It': I received a nice letter of thanks for my involvement in the making of 'Flog It' and as always I enjoyed the experience. Most of the filming was done out in the Bay, but afterwards, the team came back to Guides Farm and Olive gave them all a brew - tea not the stronger stuff – and then they did a short interview with us in the living room.

CHAPTER SEVEN

Away from the Walks

FROM GUIDES FARM TO CRUFTS

WORK AND MORE WORK seemed the norm once we had moved into Guides Farm, with Olive doing more than her fair share. One evening before going upstairs to bed I picked up the *Exchange and Mart* magazine, which we took regularly, and saw an advertisement for Chihuahua puppies for sale. I gave the Preston number a ring. A woman's voice at the other end told me about the puppies she had for sale, the price and gave me details on how to get to her house.

Olive was now excited, as she had got to know a lovely person who had bred, shown and judged these little dogs the whole of her working life – a Mrs Fearfield from Canny Hill, near Newby Bridge. She had given us several interesting books on Chihuahuas, so Olive had a fair idea of the type of dog she would have liked to own.

The very next evening it was decided that I would drive over to Preston and take our daughter, Diane, with me for company. Olive was to stay at home with the rest of the family. I was not used to driving long distances and even Preston seemed a long way to me. We eventually found the right house and the owner of the puppies answered the door. She seemed pleasant enough, although she did not ask us in and kept us waiting outside. I thought this was a bit strange after we had travelled all that way. She eventually came to the door carrying a puppy in her arms, gave it to us and took the money.

I was not an expert on Chihuahuas but thought that this one seemed much on the big side, black and tan in colour and more like a cross breed. I was really tired when we arrived back at Guides Farm. Diane must also have been tired, as she had held the puppy on her knee for the entire journey. Olive is the type of person who would never speak her mind, or say what she thought if she were to hurt someone's feelings, but when she saw the puppy we had bought I could tell that she was disappointed with it.

The next morning the puppy seemed happy enough and would probably have made a good pet, but I wanted Olive to have a Chihuahua of which she was proud. She took the new puppy outside onto the front lawn to relieve itself – and it promptly ran off with Olive hard on her heels.

The puppy ran down towards the Cart Lane railway crossing cottage and onto the railway line. Olive's friend, Eve Barrow, lived there and when Olive told her about the puppy, she immediately offered to go with her and chase it along the line, hoping that no trains would appear. Suddenly, the puppy turned and they missed it as it ran back towards the crossing cottage. Olive does not swear, but Eva called the little dog just about everything. Then all at once it stopped and Olive was able to grab it before it ran off again.

Back at Guides Farm, I talked with Olive about the puppy and decided that we should give the person where we had got it a ring. She was really abrupt with me on the phone and didn't want to know what I had to say about the puppy, but I did let her know that I would be returning it as we did not think it to be a true Chihuahua.

The following evening Diane and I made the journey back to Preston with the puppy. We soon found the house and knocked on the door several times before the husband came. He told us that his wife worked at the local pub and would not be home till late. We hadn't come all this way for nothing, so we decided to wait as long as it would take. At 10pm I knocked on the door and again it was the husband, who told us that his wife had still not come home. I think he was telling us a lie, because when he closed the door we could hear him talking to someone.

I tried the door again – knock, knock – and we got no response. We had hoped to return the puppy and get our money back, but these two horrible people had other ideas.

I was so fed up by this time that I opened their front door, put the puppy down, closed the door and drove off back to Guides Farm to meet up with Olive and the rest of the family. We had been taken for a ride – two in fact – and lost our money, but that did not deter me from finding a really genuine Chihuahua puppy for Olive.

We had learnt our lesson and now found a reputable registered breeder of Chihuahuas in Braintree, Essex. Although we could not travel all that way to look at the puppies he had for sale, he seemed really genuine and sent us photographs of them.

Olive chose a most beautiful little long-coated dog puppy from what we had seen of the photographs, and it was then agreed with the owner for him to send him up by train in a little dog box all the way from Braintree to Grange over Sands

Olive and I with our Chihuahuas at a local show in June 1974.

railway station. The times were given to us, so we would be there waiting. Olive was thrilled to bits as the platform cleared of passengers and the guard came towards us carrying this small box. Olive peered inside and saw two big eyes and a fluffy coat. He was lovely. He turned out to be such a character and loved by everyone. He was very cheeky, but so intelligent.

We named him Chico. He was ten weeks old and we had him for nineteen years. He was Kennel Club registered and when he became of age we thought about showing him. We decided that our daughter, Diane, would take him to dog training classes to get accustomed to meeting up with other dogs before taking him to a show. His first show was lovely and he looked a picture. Olive had bathed him the previous night and given him a really good brushing – including his teeth. He was entered in the 'puppy class, toy dog section' at our local Cartmel agricultural show. When Olive placed him on the table for the judge to handle, he bit his hand and brought blood. However, the judge must have taken a liking to him, as he gave him a third place and a rosette.

This was the start of things to come as Olive now had a hobby which took her away from the farm for a while, which she really did enjoy. She purchased another puppy – a bitch – and when she was old enough she bred from her. The puppies were all show standard and there seemed to be a demand for good quality stock. I enjoyed going along to the shows with Olive, and as time went on she did her share of winning with her little dogs. The large beam in the living room at Guides Farm was littered with rosettes from one end to the other – and most of these were red.

Olive was more than pleased when she showed one of her little Chihuahua bitches at Preston Guild Hall, as it won a first prize and this qualified her for Crufts. This little Chihuahua was a gem, very showy and had had many first prizes previously. The problem now was how were we going to get down to the Crufts dog show in London.

I then owned a Ford estate car which had plenty of room, so when the time arrived it was decided that the four of us – Olive, me, Jean and Paul – and the dog would travel by road to the big city. I had no idea of the mileage or how long it would take us to get there, so we set off well prepared for the journey. I put a mattress in the back of the car, and lots to eat and drink, with tit bits and fresh water for the little dog, and now we were on our way. We left Grange over Sands in high spirits. We would join the M6 motorway at Carnforth and continue down towards London. This seemed straightforward enough as the motorway was reasonably quiet, with not the same volume of traffic as today.

Our first and last stop on the journey was at a motorway service station near Warrington. Even at this early stage my eyes were beginning to feel the strain, so we all made towards the toilets to have a rinse and freshen ourselves up. Back at the car we decided to have a rest and relax before tackling the long journey ahead. However, we were all too excited so we left the service station and got back onto motorway. I drove steadily along without any problems and arrived in London around five o'clock in the morning.

It was here that we were soon lost and needed someone to give us directions to Olympia and Crufts dog show. The city was so quiet all those years ago, but luckily for us we saw a person walking along at a fast pace. I think he may have been jogging, but he was so helpful and in no time at all we arrived and had to wait about half an hour or so before the opening. The day was an experience not to be forgotten. Olive, although now feeling tired, had been placed in the show with her little dog, coming back home to Grange over Sands with a prize.

It was through keeping and showing these lovely little dogs that Olive and I made many new friends and it gave her a hobby which she simply loved. She became very knowledgeable about the breed and was asked to judge Chihuahua classes at many of the shows, but memories of the journey to London and winning a prize at Crufts were a dream come true.

Olive and her favourite Chihuahua Candy, photographed by
the soft light of a window at Guides Farm. (Peter Cherry)

The three donkeys (Banner, Snowflake and Dillon) and two Shetland ponies (Flikka and Dinkey) on which we gave hugely popular rides in the school holidays.

DONKEY AND PONY RIDES

I always loved to have a day out at Morecambe with Olive and the family when we had a free day in the summer, but this wasn't very often and on this occasion it was to be different. Dad and I had known this horse dealer in Morecambe for many years and both us and the other Flookburgh fishermen had bought horses from him to work on the sands in the past. He had donkeys and ponies on the beach each day, weather permitting, during the summer season, and it was him that we were going to see and find out as much information from him as we could before going into a new venture. He was very helpful.

At the Kents Bank end of our promenade was a small plot of land, fenced with a good access, but which did not seem to be in use. I thought this would be an ideal place to operate with two or three donkeys and maybe one or two Shetland ponies and much safer than on the sands. The council agreed for me to go ahead with this new venture, so now I had to look around for some quiet reliable animals. We had to be registered and visited by a veterinary person once a year to examine the animals, and last but not least to take out a public liability insurance.

I soon found three donkeys in a field at Roose and enquired about the owner. He was a potter dealer living in Ulverston, and he willingly sold me all three of them at a reasonable price. We named them Banner, Snowflake and Dillon, and now I was on the lookout for two small quiet Shetland ponies to join them. My dad suggested that I rang Ted, a dealer who lived at Marton near Dalton in Furness, to see if he had anything suitable. His wife answered the phone and said that Ted wouldn't be back till evening, but she would take the message.

Good news! Later that day Ted rang me back and told me he had a very good Shetland pony for sale – and if I went through to see it I would buy it. We did – and it was a little beauty, just what we needed.

I had now to go and look for another one of about the same size if possible but above all quiet and reliable. It took me a while before I came across another Shetland pony and this one was for sale at the Clitheroe Horse Sale at the Auction Mart. We gave it a good going over before it entered the ring, handled it, looked in its mouth and checked its teeth to give me an idea of its age, then lifted all four legs and examined its feet. This handling did not bother it and gave me a good idea of its temperament. Now it was up to us to find a suitable place in the sellers' ring and hope that there wouldn't be too many people interested in buying it, which would push up the price. We were lucky and the hammer went down on mine – the last bid. This little pony turned out to be as quiet as the other one, and we named them Flikka and Dinky.

I bought some saddlery and three donkey saddles on the same day and later purchased some donkey bells from a dealer in Morecambe.

The season for giving rides on these lovely little animals was only a short one, about six weeks of the school holidays, with weekends being the busiest. I had my daughter Jean and many of her friends always willing to help, as on most Sundays I would be leading a walk across the Bay, but I knew they were in safe hands. Olive and my mother and father loved to come down to what they called the Donkey Paddock, as there was always someone of interest to chat to as well as keeping all the young helpers busy and out of mischief.

As time went on I decided to purchase some larger ponies, as my daughter Jean was horse mad and thought that we could start giving pony trekking rides out from the farm. I now had to find at least six quiet, reliable ponies of the right age and suitable to do the job. Domino, a black and white pony, was bought at Clitheroe Horse Sale. Cheyenne, a palomino pony, came from Walney Island, near Barrow in Furness.

Sparky had a rough start in life. He had been abandoned on the wayside as a

Domino and Cheyenne, two of the six ponies that we acquired to do pony trekking from Guides Farm.

two year old and Lancaster City Council impounded him, then advertised for the owner to come along and claim him but no one ever did. He was put up for sale in the cattle auction at Lancaster and my father and I went along and bought him. What a super pony he turned out to be!

Bluey was a very nice Fell pony, which we bought from a dealer at Shap. Horses were being sold abroad at this time for the meat trade, so we actually saved Bluey's life and he turned out to be a belter! Next came Danny Boy, a big Dale horse who was jet black. He was a teenager and had his own ways but there was no harm in him at all.

Finally there was Minstrel, which I bought from a dealer in Morecambe. I was taken to look at him on waste ground, where he had very little to eat and no shelter and was tethered to a metal pole. I liked him as soon as I saw him and asked the dealer if I could have a ride. He unleashed the tether, slung it around Minstrel's neck and gave me a leg up. I bought him and he was delivered in a horsebox the very next day.

It was quite hard work looking after all these animals with feeding, grooming and preparing them to go out on the rides. But the young girls just loved it and, during the six weeks of school holidays, most of them almost lived with us here at the farm, with Olive making meals for all of them, and they didn't want to go home. Many of them slept over, with Olive putting mattresses down on the bedroom floors.

Sadly, nothing lasts forever and when our daughter Jean met her boyfriend and decided to get married, she was to leave home and go to live in Wales. I was now too busy on the sands to be able to keep the ponies and continue to give rides. It is a sad time, when you have had animals and worked with them and got to know their ways and they also get to know you, and then you have to see them go. Luckily, they all went to very good homes – well not all of them. We kept Domino and Cheyenne till the end of their days and they are both buried on the farm.

I have always been a horse lover and at the present time we have a really good sort of cob called Charlie, who is broken to harness. I drove him in the private driving class at the local Cartmel agricultural show in August 2008. We also own two Shetland ponies.

Cartmel Show in August 2008 saw me in proper regalia handling our 14,2 hand cob Charlie. With me is Mike Carter, a local friend who regularly used to come out on the sands.

I have always had an affinity with horses and ponies, as can be seen when back in 1963 I posed in front of Guides Farm with baby Jean riding bareback.

BIRDS OF THE BAY

Morecambe Bay is one of our most important habitats for birdwatchers. Wildfowl and waders descend in their tens of thousands and many other groups are drawn by the abundance of readily available food and by the safe resting and nesting sites provided by the sheltered shores and islands. The Bay is also the most important wintering site in the United Kingdom for oystercatchers – local name 'sea-a-pie' – and dunlin. The smallest and quickest moving of birds when they are feeding on the sands, dunlin are known by the fisher folk, including myself, as 'mice'.

The most striking feature of Morecambe Bay in terms of birdlife is its size. It is the second largest bay in the United Kingdom after the Wash, but it has the greatest area of inter-tidal sands and mudflats. Seven rivers feed into the Bay. The Leven is the overspill from Windermere, and the Crake runs into the upper reaches at Greenodd near Ulverston . The Kent starts up the valley above Kentmere and then winds its way south through Staveley and Kendal and into the upper reaches of the Bay at Sandside. Here it is meets the Bela river and meanders from one side of the sandy reaches to the other, finding its own course towards Arnside, then through the railway viaduct and out into the Bay on the east side. The Winster enters at Grange, the Keer at Carnforth, and the Lune adds to these at the mouth of the Bay.

All of these rivers are tidal to some extent, mainly on the lower reaches, but sediment brought down into the estuary with heavy rainfall and high tides is deposited on the mudflats and makes good feeding grounds for the birds of the Bay. These are mainly shelduck and the greylag geese, which stay on the estuary very close to Guides Farm for most of the winter. Gulls include the common gull, the lesser black- backed gull and the herring gull – the commonest of the three.

Oystercatcher – a fairly large black and white bird – used to be so numerous in the Bay that the fishermen of Flookburgh were allowed to set nets to catch them. They were called fly nets and were set out on the sands at low tide, just before the rising tide. On the first rise the birds were moved by the tide and always flew along the edge of the water, where the fly nets caught them in quantity. Most of the village fishermen would set these nets and the birds were taken to the open markets at Barrow, Ulverston and Kendal, where was always good trade for them. They are now protected and I love to hear and watch them out there on what has been described as 'The Wet Sahara'.

Dunlin are not seen quite so often at this side of the Bay, but I still see these fascinating little birds way out on the sands when I am setting my fluke nets. Sometimes when I am out there alone, miles from anywhere, I will suddenly hear the sound of thousands of wings and see them wheeling and turning. This mass of birds will form a cloud of a forever changing shape. In the sunlight they are so beautiful that you never quite get used to the sight and have to stop work for a few minutes to watch. When they are down on the sand feeding, they do indeed run like mice.

Taking off again to fresh ground, they are so close-knit and all together in flight. It is a miracle to watch as they rise and fall and weave about, looking at first glance like a cloud of smoke blowing in the air. Then, suddenly, the colour changes to silver, giving the impression of a huge mass of tinsel flickering from the sun's reflections. Close to, they fly past with the sound and movement of air, but with such force that it is hard to realise they have no mechanical means of propulsion. When they turn, they appear to be all one, so close together but yet not touching. This cloud of little birds is like a genie being released from a magic lamp. One second it is silver, then it is black. Almost a miracle!

A newcomer to this side of the Bay, which can be seen almost every day on what is now marshland, is the snow-white egret. There have also been sightings of bitterns – three of them twenty-five yards from the shore – when we had the very hard frosts for quite a long spell. Food must have been scarce for them in their own habitat.

When our daughter Diane was about eleven years old, she often used to come to the beach and wait for me on my return from the fishing nets. She loved to ride on the tractor across the railway, when the gates would be opened specially for us. Sometimes there would be the added thrill of waiting for a train to go past before the crossing keeper could open them. On such a day Diane was waiting on the beach when, just as I was coming up to her, she saw four little ducklings plaintively calling for their mother, who never came. She called me over and we collected the fluffy little creatures and carried them back to Guides Farm.

They could only have been a few days old, and our first thoughts centred on how to keep them warm. Olive decided that the best thing to use would be the electric clothes drier. We put them on a cosy blanket in the drier, which had to be turned on and off at regular intervals to avoid extremes of temperature. This had to be done even through the night! We fed them on pieces of worms and tiny scraps of raw fish. They thrived and grew and were very content with their new mother, sleeping peacefully between feeding times.

We used to fill a shallow bath with water and as they grew, they enjoyed swimming around. They had a wonderful time diving for little pieces of bread that Diane threw in for them. But as time went on we realised they were needing their freedom, as they were starting to fly around in the living room, so we took them down to the beach. They were not the four little balls of fluff anymore, but four young mallards able to fend for themselves and no longer in need of us.

I have seen shelduck with their young running about on the sands, but rarely have I seen mallards doing the same. I think they like to nest well away from the sea and more often nearer to freshwater.

Swallows come to nest in the outbuildings of Guides Farm every year and they are always a welcome sight. Olive says that they bring us good luck. I don't know about that, but they are a pleasure to watch, flying in and out of the buildings without fear.

It has been said that there are now fewer sparrows to be seen. Here at the farm we have great numbers of both house and hedge sparrows. They are very tame and seem to know when it is their mealtime, as Olive enjoys feeding them from the front door first thing in the morning. Coming so close and getting used to her, they do not seem to have any fear at all. At one stage last year, one sparrow followed Olive and hopped its way into the kitchen. As she got it some food and spoke to it, the sparrow just followed her back to the front door and waited to be fed! I am amazed to watch them as they do not fear us at all.

We have numerous blackbirds and one particularly stands out as it has a broken foot and has been seen here for the last five years. In the wintertime, the robin appears to be much tamer and comes up close to be fed. It is so easy at times like these to be prepared with a camera and I am sure it is possible to take close-up shots. The blue tits visit the bird table, but are so quick and gone in a flash.

I have noticed for the past few years that we have a tiny wren nesting in the wall of one of the outbuildings. It is a joy to see this tiny bird as they seem quite rare these days.

WEATHER IN THE BAY

The weather plays a big part in bringing about changes we have seen during the past forty-six years at Guides Farm. The spring of 1983 was the wettest on record and brought dramatic changes. Mood in the Bay can alter minute by minute, but nothing had prepared me for what I was to see. It had rained solidly all the previous day and, although it was now fine for the first time, visibility was poor with hazy conditions and the air was very humid. I was now witnessing something I had never seen in my lifetime and realised that the River Kent had moved dramatically away from the Grange side of the Bay. It was now running towards the Silverdale, Jenny Brown's Point and Carnforth Marsh side of the Bay and very close to Priest Skeer – a rocky outcrop about half a mile out from Bolton-le-Sands.

Encountering changes so great can be a bit scary at the time, with the River Kent at its peak in full spate from the previous rainfall and like a roaring sea. Every now and again, huge chunks of sand embankments would topple into the bed of the river due to the very fast flow. The whole situation was becoming very eerie. From the marshland there was a drop into the riverbed of at least ten feet. At times like these, there is just no way one could organise a cross-Bay walk until the river had settled itself down.

Morecambe Bay is still an amazing place. Anyone who ventures out onto the apparently endless expanses of sand cannot help but be impressed and even overwhelmed by the vastness of the surroundings. At high tide the Bay can be deceptively calm, but in reality it is an extremely dynamic place. Tidal bores can roar over the sands at nine knots – the fisherman's term and mine is 'as fast as a horse can gallop'. These powerful tides move tons of sand, building up banks, gouging out deep and muddy channels and scraping out 'melgraves' (deep holes) that fill with quicksand and change daily.

A strong wind coinciding with a high tide can play havoc, hurling great waves, smashing embankments and moving large areas of the salt marsh away. These are living sands and always on the move. At the moment the River Kent appears to be taking away a large proportion of the marsh opposite Grange. Residents in the town will be pleased, but it could be quite some time before you again get the Kent close to the shore.

There is nothing worse than when fog envelopes the Bay, but luckily this rarely happens during the walking season. We can still get days with misty rain, making visibility very poor, but I find the walkers usually keep closely knit together, which makes it much easier for me.

The last walk of the 2008 season saw the worst conditions one can get out in the Bay with a Force 10 gale and the rain coming at us like bullets. Despite all that punishment, many of the walkers thanked me as they left the shore at Kent's Bank and I never heard a grumble.

A few summers ago I arranged to take a small group of about twenty walkers across the Leven estuary and out to Chapel Island. We all met on the shore at Sandgate on the most beautiful hot day. Most of the group were teenagers with the idea of having a swim as the tides had left a deep pool close to the rocks at the seaward end of the island. Others wanted to explore and have a picnic.

It takes about an hour to walk out to the island, and we expected to spend about the same time out there before leaving for home and the shore at Sandgate. We got everyone together and set off when suddenly we could hear a noise away in the distance, almost like the sound of the tidal bore or an express steam train. It was a storm moving up the Bay towards us very fast and it really did look frightening. As it reached us, the raindrops were hitting us like bullets from a gun, with lightning striking all around us on the wet sand. The noise of the storm was so great that it seemed an age from me blowing my whistle to the group hearing it, as they all had their heads down and moving at the same time but in

Weather has a direct effect on the tidal bore in Morecambe Bay, which can roar over the sands at nine knots and move tons of material in a matter of moments. (Paul Nickson)

the wrong direction. We had been on lovely dry sand, due to the tides being low and the weather warm, but now there was water everywhere and this made it more frightening.

Eventually the storm eased and we could then see where we were going but we all thought that we had had a very lucky escape. It was probably the most frightening experience of a lifetime for every one of us that day.

LOST – AND FOUND

In 1977 I was very pleased when John Duerdon of Arnside Coastguard asked me if I would be interested in joining their Auxiliary Service reporting station. I readily agreed and was officially enrolled.

I have been called upon many times to assist the police and, although they do a wonderful job, they are not trained to go out onto the sands. I had this phone call from Penrith Police headquarters, telling me of a very worrying incident on the sands at Humphrey Head, and would I get down there as soon as possible? On arriving, there seemed to be policemen everywhere. It was right in the holiday season and the weather was good. People with their cars had come from the South Lakeland Holiday Leisure Park at Flookburgh. There must have been up to eight vehicles, which had been driven down to Humphrey Head on reasonably dry sand, reversed as close to the rocks as possible and parked up for a picnic.

The area was a suntrap and the visitors had no idea of the sands and tides. A policeman came over to me and I told him who I was and the phone call I had received. He said that a couple with their two young children had parked down there and he pointed to the vehicle furthest away, and then told me that whilst the parents were having a nap the two children – brother and sister – had wandered off. The parents were so upset and the mother was sobbing uncontrollably.

The father had set off in his car to look for them. He had only got about three hundred yards away from where he was parked when he got the car stuck in the mud. I asked the policeman if I could have a word with the parents to ascertain the children's whereabouts when they were last seen. They pointed in a south-westerly direction. I was now relieved, as what they thought was the incoming tide was in fact a mirage. Hot weather and dry sands can give this effect. I could now assure the parents that what they were looking at was not the tide, and if the children had wandered in that direction I could not see them coming to much harm.

The sands were dry for miles as far as the eye could see and the tide would not cover them again for at least two days. I am used to looking long distances out there, and I thought I could make out something moving and mentioned this to the policeman. He took a look through his binoculars and agreed but could not make it out to be a person. He had his Volvo estate parked on hard standing near the road. I thought we could get out there with that vehicle, so I suggested we start out and drive across the sands.

"Oh no!" he said, "I cannot take my vehicle out there."

"No," I said, "You can't, but if I jump in with you – you can."

He did not hesitate and off we set, with me giving him instruction to avoid the dykes and gullies and eventually we travelled miles over firm dry sand.

The policeman could hardly believe what was happening now being a few miles out from the land. As we got nearer, we could see that it was the young girl and, although we were in a police vehicle, she was as pleased to see us as we were to see her. When questioned, she told us that she and her brother had fallen out with each other and he had made for the shore towards the Lakeland Leisure Centre, which is where they were staying.

The policeman now let his colleagues at Humphrey Head know that we had found the young girl, and arranged for someone to travel to the Lakeland Centre to see if they could locate the young lad. He was found in a very short time and, when the parents were told that they were both safe and sound, they couldn't thank us enough. A tractor had to be brought to pull their car from the soft mud. Luckily it was not the dangerous quicksand and the recovery was not difficult, so all was now well that ended well. But had the tides been running much higher, the outcome could have been quite different.

I think the worst times when you have been brought up to follow the sands are when there has been a loss of life in the Bay. These tragedies hit us the worst, especially when knowing the moods of the Bay and what can happen out there with the fast running tides and quicksand.

Luckily there is now more rescue coverage with the coastguard and lifeboat stations around the Bay. Morecambe, Ulverston, Flookburgh, and Arnside are equipped with the right kind of transport to access the Bay at most points in an emergency, although the Maritime and Coastguard Agency removed the boat from Arnside Coastguard in 2008, prompting thousands of people to put their name to a petition calling for it to be reinstated.

Happily, in May 2009 the Agency gave in and now the station has jet skis and two Argo 'cats' – amphibious vehicles with specialist tracked wheels. The jet skis will be the first to be used in an estuary and the Argo will provide more flexibility. Tim Farron, the MP for Westmorland and Lonsdale, has said that he still thinks a boat is needed to complete the kit and allow a large-scale operation to take place. Only time will tell.

CHAPTER EIGHT

Looking Back

MUM AND DAD

MY MOTHER AND FATHER (I called them mum and dad) just loved coming down to Guides Farm after their retirement to help us out in the fish house in the winter months, sorting the whitebait and packing it for Young's Seafoods. In the summer holidays they would go down onto the donkey paddock on the promenade, with mum taking the money for the rides. Olive and Jean gave me a hand putting youngsters on the ponies and donkeys and dad, walking round with a stick in his hand, kept an eye on the animals. They found enjoyment meeting up with so many people from away and having a chat with them. On one occasion mum was so pleased. She could not believe she was talking to 'Eelie' from television. He came along the promenade to the donkey paddock and had a chat with both mum and dad. It made their day.

When I was rushed into Furness General Hospital at Barrow with a suspected detached retina of my left eye, my mum was suddenly taken ill and was also rushed by ambulance to the same hospital. She died aged 77 on 1 September 1989 at the same time as I was having my operation. The consultant ophthalmic surgeon, Mr Ian Hubbard, asked Olive not to tell me, as I would have been terribly upset and this would have disturbed my eye with disastrous consequences. I was therefore not told of mum's death until three days later.

This coincidence was covered by the *Barrow News and Mail*, which related how we were both in the hospital at the same time. I was unable to attend mum's

My dad had a wonderful life, living at Flookburgh until the age of 101 and latterly buying a dog, a Shetland pony and some laying hens for company.

funeral as I was confined to bed at Guides Farm on medical advice. Family and friends came along to the farm after the funeral and all of them came and sat at my bedside. It felt good to see them.

Mum and dad had a good life together. They were both hard workers until their retirement, but mum was good at baking and making splendid meals so we knew that dad was going to find it hard for a while. Villagers thought he would never manage on his own. Olive suggested that he came to Guides Farm to stay with us for a while. This he did but not for long, as he said that if he stayed away from his own home for too long he would find it harder to go back. He eventually moved back home, buying himself a dog for company and also a Shetland pony to keep the grass down in the paddock as well as some laying hens. These kept him busy and occupied.

As he was born in Flookburgh, people just loved to sit with him and listen to his stories of past and present. He had a remarkable memory. His hobby was listening to the radio and he even made his own recordings of old songs. He recorded with me several times for radio, and was written about and photographed many times. Hannah Hauxwell, the well-known and famous lady of the Yorkshire Dales, loved to visit dad and sit and reminisce with him when she came to stay with us for a week's holiday.

Dad died on 5 April, 2006, aged 101 years, just weeks from his 102nd birthday. He was special – a life that touched so many people's lives that he will never be forgotten. A day never passed without us being in touch with one another. He was always interested in the cross-Bay walks and the cockling in the Bay. His is sadly missed.

SETBACKS IN LIFE

One is lucky in life to get away without having some form of illness or other. In 1984, late on after the walking season had finished, I was fishing the Bay for whitebait, which involved setting nets and lifting very heavy iron bars from the sand. I became very lame and in pain with sciatica.

My doctor said that I had a slipped disc and would need hospital treatment. I had heard of people with the same complaint getting almost instant relief from a physiotherapist. I only tried this once and that was enough for me. I travelled all the way to Preston, laid on a table and was hit in my disc area three times with a wooden hammer. I came home feeling much worse than when I went in.

I therefore followed my doctor's advice and was admitted to Kendal hospital. This was the old hospital and the treatment was almost the same. Lying flat, my affected leg was attached to heavy weights, which dangled over the edge of the bed and were supposed to stretch the muscles and put everything back into place. I was in the hospital for one week and after that time I expected I would be able to run back to Guides Farm but this was not the case. It took me a while but when spring came along I was feeling much better and stronger. I was looking forward to getting out on the sands again and leading my walks.

In 1989, as already related, I suffered a detached retina. I had organised more than twenty cross-Bay walks for charity that year, which had been undertaken in spite of acute pain and loss of vision in my left eye. It had been the best summer for Bay walks since I became Guide and I was determined not to let down any of the charitable organisations, although I was feeling a bit handicapped and worried. Just a few days before I had to go into hospital, I led the Mayor of Grange 'Foresight Appeal' walk from Arnside to Kents Bank when more than £1,000 was raised for a glaucoma monitoring machine at Furness General Hospital.

I have had no reoccurrence of that terrible pain, but in 1994 I did have a setback when I underwent heart by-pass surgery. My family, that is my beloved wife, Olive, and at that time, five grown up children and nine grandchildren, were not sure if I would pull through, but the lord must have been on my side. Not only have I recovered, but now eat a healthy diet, feel fitter than most men of my age and still lead a very busy active life on the sands during the summer months – although I must say I have some very good helpers.

On the afternoon of 12 May 2008 I was working in the yard, not very far from the house, when I heard Olive shouting "Ced, Ced" as loud as she could. I found her stood near the front door of the house leaning back against the wall and she was covered in blood. A friend from Leeds had been to visit us, and had mistakenly left her mobile phone on the kitchen table. Olive went to try to catch her before she drove off and ran down the garden path, suddenly tripping and flying head first into our heavy metal gate.

She was feeling very faint, so I rang 999 and asked for an ambulance. I was told that there was not one available in Grange, but one would come from Kendal and would be with us in about half an hour. In the meantime I rang our daughter Jean at Flookburgh, but she was very upset and said she would ring Christine Bennet, one our best friends who lives in Grange. She was here in a flash and we got Olive into the house and settled her on the settee.

No matter how much pressure we put on Olive's head, we could not stem the blood. The three large towels we used got absolutely sodden with blood, which was all over the furniture. Poor Olive thought her time had come. When the ambulance eventually arrived, Christine offered to travel with Olive, as I had a cross-Bay walk organised for later in the afternoon. They took her to Westmorland General and found that she could not be attended to there, so she was then rushed by road to Lancaster Infirmary with the sirens going and being told all the time not to worry.

At Lancaster they were absolutely marvellous with Olive. As the wound was so bad, she was worried about losing her hair, but they told her they would only cut off what was necessary. Olive had eighteen stitches and eight clips, and the wound healed marvellously. I travelled to Lancaster that evening after the walk to visit Olive, but she was not too well and, although she was so pleased to see me, she was very upset.

She was kept in hospital a few days and then I drove through and brought her home to Guides Farm, along with the tablets that had been prescribed for her. On 28 May I came home from the sands to find Olive ill in her chair. I phoned the doctor, then the ambulance and she was taken to Westmorland General Hospital. I had to ring the hospital the next day after 11am to see how she was faring. I was terribly worried about her.

By 2 June we were all still worried and my daughter Jean rang the hospital and spoke to a nurse. She said that Olive had been hallucinating through the night, but she was now having her breakfast. The nurse thought that the hallucinating might be due to the tablets that she had been taking and she would mention this to the doctor. When we went to visit Olive later that day she was feeling much better and, on seeing her, so was I. We all had a good laugh.

The nurse said that they would probably keep her in hospital for about another three days to monitor her tablets. She eventually came home, her tablets were changed and she was soon doing really well and keeping very busy.

ACCOLADES AND AWARDS

Such have been our setbacks but we have many wonderful memories of happier occasions. Olive and I would not want to change anything that has happened here over all the years that I have been the Sands Guide. Our lives have been enriched with meeting and making friends with so many people from different walks of life.

Many publications have shown interest in our way of life. The list seems endless – *Cumbria, Lancashire Life, Country Walking In Britain*, the *Times* magazine and newspaper, *Country Life, Lakeland Walker* and *Springbok*, which featured fantastic photographs but I could not read the story as it was in some foreign language. It may have been Dutch, but to me was more like double Dutch! There have also been such magazines as *Islands, Land Rover, Weekend, You* (the *Mail on Sunday* magazine) and, last but certainly not least, *OK* with its ultimate accolade of a feature article following the royal carriage crossing in May 1985.

In 1989 I was given the honorary degree of Master of Science and Technology at Lancashire Polytechnic, now the University of Central Lancashire. Both Olive and I always look forward to attending the award ceremonies at the university, where I take my place in the procession at the Guild Hall and Olive as a VIP sits with the audience. In 1996 I was awarded the honorary degree of Master of Science at Lancaster University. Two years later I received 'The Bernard Gooch Award as Cumbria Personality of the Year for services to tourism.'

In 1999 I was awarded the MBE by Her Majesty the Queen at Buckingham Palace. I received many letters of congratulation including one from the lady in waiting to Princess Alexandra. It stated that the Princess was delighted to see my name in the Queen's Birthday Honours List. She had happy memories of her fascinating chat with me over lunch at Lancaster University and sent me her best wishes.

I was surprised and pleased to receive an invitation to a service in the Priory Church at Lancaster to commemorate the 600th anniversary of the link between the Crown and Duchy of Lancaster. The service was to take place on 23 July in the presence of the Queen, Duke of Lancaster and Prince Philip, Duke of Edinburgh. It was disappointing that only one ticket was issued to each invitee, as I believe this is the only occasion when Olive has not been at my side.

I was also invited to attend the Royal Luncheon, which was held in Lancaster Town Hall, following the service at the Priory. The Queen was on table 1 and the Duke of Edinburgh on table 2, along with myself and eight other guests, including Jean Bartholomew, the widow of Eric Morecambe.

In the same year I won the Barclays Bank prize with *Sand Pilot of Morecambe Bay* in the Lakeland Book of the Year competition. I have enjoyed writing all my books and have been thrilled at having them published, along with the feedback and enquiries from overseas about the Bay. I believe that the royal family have them in their libraries

A most beautiful book was published in 1999 entitled *Keepers of the Kingdom: the ancient offices of Britain,* by Alistair Bruce, Julian Calder and Mark Cator. The *Daily Mail* of 18 February 2000 reviewed the book and concluded: 'Of all the Queen's men, the Queen's Guide across the shifting sands of Morecambe Bay is perhaps the most useful service of them all'.

I met Julian Calder when he came up from London by train to Grange over Sands. It was a really nice summer's day, and when I arrived home from the sands after fishing my nets, Olive was plying him with tea and biscuits. After being introduced, we made our way back onto the sands via Kents Bank railway station and went way out into the Bay to take shots of me for the new book.. We seemed to be out there for ages and, as the light started to go, Julian as photographer lit up his lamp on a tall stand. He seemed pleased with what he had got and we eventually set off back for Guides Farm.

We didn't hear from him again until the following summer and this time it was a phone call from Balmoral. He said he had Alistair Bruce, the author of the book, with him and they would like to go out onto the sands again to take more photographs. They duly took more shots of the Bay, with me as Guide putting the 'brobs' markers down into the sand. They were more than pleased with what they took and I later received a copy of the book, which Alistair had signed for us. His inscription read:

Cedric and Olive

You have both been quite marvellous.

No Duke of Lancaster has ever been better served
By a Guide over Kent Sands, nor has a Duke's husband ever
been more pleased to see that this writer knew your name!

With very best wishes and thanks,

Alistair

I heard from him again in 2000, as I had previously written to him to ask if he would kindly write a foreword for my book *Sand Walker*. He duly obliged and later told me that he had been invited to Balmoral to have dinner with the Queen and thought it would be a good idea to present her with a copy of my book. The Queen accepted and thanked Alistair for *Sand Walker*, which is now in the library at Balmoral.

In March 2001 I received a Civic Award in 'recognition and sincere appreciation for services rendered to the community, life and well being of the citizens of Granger over Sands'. I was given the Morecambe Bay Partnership Award in September 2002 and both Olive and I were granted Honorary Life Memberships.

The Golden Eagle Award of the Outdoor Writers Guild was presented to me in 2003 for services to the community. The Lancashire, Blackpool Tourism Awards in 2008-2009 saw me honoured as a 'Tourism Ambassador' for leading walks across Morecambe Bay. It was an absolutely wonderful occasion at the Eawood Park Football Stadium at Blackburn.

Another memorable ceremony was at the local pub Guide over Sands, when

Olive and I were proud to be given Honorary Life Membership of the Morecambe Bay
Partnership in 2002. (Furness Newspapers)

Moorhouses sales executive David Slane announced: 'The brewery is absolutely delighted to brew a beer in Cedric's honour to mark the outstanding contribution he has made to the Grange over Sands area over his long career.'

It has given me great pleasure over all these years to have conducted thousands of people across the sands and in many cases contributed to raising millions of pounds for charity. I felt it was really something to be asked to contribute a recipe to a Celebrity Cook Book with the following names: David Beckham, Chris Tarrant, Gary Rhodes, Delia Smith, Kevin Keegan, Alex Ferguson, Richard and Judy, Terry Wogan, Carol Vorderman, Nigella Lawson, Richard Whiteley, Jamie Oliver, Cherie Booth and Gloria Hunniford.

My recipe was as follows:

The Sauce

You will need a quarter of a pound of cooked fresh shrimps –
Morecambe Bay if possible.

Wash them well in cold water. Pop in a pan on gentle heat,
Add a knob of butter, a touch of salt and pepper,
A touch of English mustard
A half teaspoon of Demerara sugar and a dash of paprika.

As the ingredients start to simmer,
Add a touch of corn flour and a little milk.
Bring to the boil and take off the heat and let it stand .
For special occasions you can liquidise with fresh cream.

Fluke or Flounder fillets

You will need approximately 1lb of fish fillets.
Cover with seasoned flour.
Shallow pan fry in oil for 2 – 3 minutes, turning once.

Garnish round the edges with chopped yellow peppers,
Finely chopped onion and cucumber and a squeeze of lemon.

It is now ready to serve.

A meal fit for a Queen!

A happy moment, pulling the first pint of beer named after me at the Guide over Sands public house in Grange. Watching the proceedings is Larry Bennett.

Last words

GUIDES FARM is still a very busy household with much happening. A large diary is kept and looked at each day, with its bookings for the walks and for schoolchildren to be taken out into the Bay to learn about the environment, bird life and the fishing methods. They all seem to enjoy themselves.

There is still a wide interest in the Bay among journalists, who arrange to come along to the farm and sit alongside me with a recorder. The Bay is also the perfect location for photographers to come along and capture the ever-changing sands, tides and quicksand. There are few places to equal its beautiful sunrises and sunsets, which are surely a photographer's dream.

The tides run into the Bay twice in twenty-four hours, with one week of high tides, followed by a week of low tides. That is the pattern throughout the year. From late April till the end of September my time on the low tide week is taken up with the walks. On the high tides I set my nets to catch the tasty fluke (flounder). The season for catching flukes begins in May, although they come up into the Bay earlier than that if they have been down in deeper and warmer waters for the winter months, spawned and are hungry to feed on the young cockles, named 'whee-at'. The fish come in on the tide and don't have very long to feed on some of the higher sand banks, but these areas are amass with food and the fluke soon begin to put on weight. They are a very tasty fish. I still enjoy setting my nets and catching the fish as we eat lots to keep us healthy, although filleting them does take up a lot of my time.

As part of our routine, Olive shares the burden of answering the phone, which sometimes is hectic with up to forty calls a day. We also meet up with many people passing by, especially holiday makers who want to have a chat.

From late April until September my time is taken up with cross-Bay walks on the low tides, but on the high tides I am busy fishing. These views show me leaving Guides Farm with the tractor and all its paraphernalia; re-setting whitebait nets out in the Bay; and inserting stakes for the fluke nets with daughter Jean. (Peter Cherry)

Olive handles up to forty phone enquiries a day regarding the cross-Bay walks.

First thing in the morning, we make a brew. Olive prefers coffee and I like a cup of tea. We then have to attend to the fire. The living room at Guides Farm is fairly big and it is not easy in the colder winter months to keep in the heat. I always keep a good fire going and can get through quite a lot of coal during the winter. This is not a cheap fuel any more as it now sells at £270 per ton. We keep warm in the bathroom with a Calor gas heater and also have the use of one in the kitchen when needed.

The animals have to be fed twice a day when they are still inside, but will be turned out to grass as the weather becomes warmer. We rear a few beef cattle from baby calves, starting them off on milk powder, which is quite hard work, but we are used to it and keep them till they are two years old. We are always sad when the time comes for them to go to the auction mart, but whilst they have been here at the farm they have had a 'Life of Riley'. They are almost like our pets, so if we think about it that way it does not seem quite so bad.

I have a love of animals. We have a British Sein goat – who lives, sleeps and feeds with the ponies that I have already mentioned as they do not like to be parted. We also keep a few hens up in the orchard. Brown eggers – with no lions stamped on them!

Roe deer come onto the land at Guides Farm and locals like to see them. They breed and have their young in a quiet sheltered position in the meadows. One year a neighbour rang us here at the farm and asked if we had seen the baby deer. She said it was no bigger than a Yorkshire terrier dog and was following behind the parents, crossing over the field behind the farm from the orchard where it had probably been born. It was such a wonderful sight!

As soon as it becomes dusk, we are always glad to watch out for bats which live in the barn. They are about the size of a swallow and sweep backwards and forwards without flying very far from the barn.

Letters come to Guides Farm to ask if I give lectures on Morecambe Bay. I do and always enjoy sharing my favourite subject with an audience. Olive accompanies me and is my experienced projectionist. I think I will be right in saying that we can compete with any of the modern digital presentations. Our show is humorous and can run for up to one and a half hours. At the end of a recent show a member of the audience came up to me and said, "Mr. Robinson, if you hadn't been Queen's Guide over the Sands, you would have made a very good comedian!"

I don't know about that, although I do really enjoy myself. It is teamwork by the two of us, but I still think I was born to the sands. For almost twenty-five years, I led the walks from Hest Bank and Morecambe Lodge Farm across the Bay to Grange.

In those first few years following my appointment, the walks were hardly known compared with today, and only took place at weekends and then only on a Sunday. No one wanted a Saturday walk, as most people worked until Saturday lunchtime then. The walk took no longer than three hours, coming ashore at the Grange side of the Bay at Grange over Sands railway station or sometimes at the Bathing Pool on the promenade, whichever was the most suitable place at the time.

I had never heard of the walks personally and I only lived a few miles away. Very rarely did one see children on the walk with their parents. Although the dates fixed for these walks were advertised in the local press, they were still relatively unknown to

The hens that we keep up in the orchard are 'brown eggers' – with no lions stamped on them! (Paul Nickson – 2)

outsiders and those who did take part in a walk seemed to be of a similar age group. Computers changed all that.

It is totally different today. People have more leisure time on their hands, with a shorter working week and now walking the sands is a national pastime. Seasons vary so much as do the tides, but between late April and late September about 10,000 people of all ages share this wonderful experience in the season. And I usually am able to choose up to thirty weekend dates, as well as some during the week.

A key factor that has contributed to the ever-increasing popularity of the cross-Bay walk is its success as a means of fund raising, with some groups now numbering five hundred. Walking is encouraged to help people keep fitter, healthier and live longer. I can definitely agree with that. After my double heart by-pass operation in 1994, the doctors told me that I was not an invalid but should stick to a sensible diet. When I felt fit enough I was to get out onto those sands and do what I did best – walking across the Bay and meeting up with all those lovely people. I took their advice and have long been back on my feet and leading from the front – and not riding on a tractor as many people think. As each new season approaches, I still get that feel good factor after all these years. Is it something in the air, or maybe the water, or that little tot of whisky that Olive and I take regularly as a nightcap? Who knows!

Morecambe Bay remains a magical place and I shall never cease to enjoy the spectacle of its magnificent sunsets. (Paul Nickson)

APPENDIX

Even Shrimps Love Brass Band Music

By Tiberius

The following was sent on to me by W R Mitchell MBE.

John Firth, Latrobe, Tasmania, was prompted to write this piece for me when his sister, who lives in Harrogate, visited him in Tasmania and took with her my book *One Man's Morecambe Bay* and it delighted him.

"I am Elvis, the Morecambe Bay Shrimp. I move about in the murky waters of the first channel, near Morecambe Promenade. My usual beat is between the Stone Jetty and the Central Pier. I get the best of two worlds of music. I get all the visiting brass bands and the continuous dance music the likes of Jack Hilton and Victor Sylvester and their bands. My favourite game is to lie doggo in the sandy sea-bed and listen to the music. Sound travels wonderfully well through calm water.

But I have to be very wary of the modern day motorised trawlers that come thundering overhead and decimate our tribe with their 18ft wide travel nets.

My Grandfather was almost caught in one of those dreadful nets. The line of wooden bobbins rolled over him whilst sleeping in the mud, which caused him to leap upwards in alarm and in great anger. The trawl-beam with net had already passed overhead, held up there by the skid frames at each end of the trawl-beam. Grandfather started swimming away as fast as he could, but was slowly sinking backwards towards the fluke-end of the net, with every second.

Then a wonderful thing happened allowing him to make a marvellous escape. The net ceased to travel due to a large weight of sand and seaweed and the propeller up above was only holding the rope tight. At full tide the sand held in suspension falls, thus levelling out the ripples. The bobbins cease to jostle and the trawler men can feel no vibrations on the trawl rope, then after a pause of 20 minutes the ripples form again. Grandfather made his escape, not knowing the amount of leeway at his disposal, with all haste. "Is the net swarping Teddy?" Grandfather heard Robert Woodhouse say to Ted Gerrard. Then came a change in direction of the trawler as the net was winched in and hurled on deck by the tackling after some of the sand was washed away.

The Morecambe Trawlers are from 30 to 32ft long, with an 8ft-6inch beam and a 4ft-6inch draught. In earlier times they were sail driven, having a bowsprit and two fore sails, a main sail and upper mainsail. At one period in their development they featured a drop keel. Then when running in close to the edge of the channel where shrimps love to laze in the warm shallows, the boats would raise the keel-board and run in even closer. For shrimps, life was always dangerous. The same for mice who dare to sample cheese on mousetraps.

But Elvis decided life was safer nearer to where the trawlers had their anchorage. However when the trawlers were fitted with the world famous Kelvin paraffin engines, the boats then favoured the deep keel that gave the propeller a constant bite in the water.

This was both good and bad for the shrimp tribe, sure, it made it safer in the shallows, but made life very dangerous in deep water.

Another feature about the shrimp boats is the false stern, besides giving more space for the net it serves to lift the boat over a stern sea when riding at anchor when the tide runs from the opposite direction. Just imagine a lady's dancing slipper, the toe is turned upside down and joined on the transom (that's the wide board at the stern of a boat). The danger period is when the boats turn with the tide and swing through 180 degrees on their moorings. Sometimes a beam-sea will flood the cockpit and put the trawler down with us. Then we go along to view the shrimp boiler where hundreds of thousands of our tribe have been boiled alive. This does not include the little ones, they get thrown to the seagulls flying just behind the boat, and we shudder to hear their greedy hollering as the small fry goes overboard. There are all kinds of tiny flat fish that come through the riddle, some have the digestive and reparatory organs on the left side of the vertebrae and others on the right. Sometimes they catch a skate more than two feet across the wings. Not forgetting those deadly fang-fish with their poisonous barbs. To save a sunken trawler from splitting wide open at the bows, the men arrive with buckets and lower the water in the boat faster than the tide recedes.

My purpose in staying close to the old jetty and Leisureland on September 28th 1979 was to hear the Tasmanian Band.

The sound waves were coming under the sand better than any telephone system. I tell you a brass band beats that honky-tonk fairground music and the continuous dance records from the Central Pier, and this was none other than the Latrobe Federal Band. Having come 11,000 miles to play a concert near to where Thomas Ward and Co had a ship-breaking yard. It was a treat for holiday makers to come to the seaside to see men at work even if they were cutting up the Majestic that once held the Atlantic Blue Ribbon. Later in 1919 three captured U-boats were cut up for scrap. They were the U96, U52 and U9. The last ship was broken up in 1931 and in 1936 the super swimming stadium was opened, which is now a leisure complex. This area which once was shrimp and periwinkle territory now has its unique compensations.

I really have a soft spot for that Tasmanian Band because up there in the Tasmanian Highlands in the shallow rock pools filled with snow water live our distant cousins Anaspides Tasmaniac, otherwise the Tasmanian mountain shrimp, once found in North America and Europe before becoming extinct.

Once upon a time, the Lancashire towns had a rota system in order to spread the holiday season, for the benefit of the boarding house keepers, so that the visitors all could have boiled cabbage throughout the season.

The landladies all boil the cabbage and strained off the juice and poured it down the drain, this giving Morecambe Bay a most wonderful flavour for 13 weeks. Let me explain also that every year when it is Bolton holidays the rain clouds come direct from the Caribbean, poor Bolton, usually they get five and a half days of rain. At first a little rain came, and then MORE –CAM(B)E. And that's how the place got its name.

Two railway companies competed which one could get passengers to the seaside at the lowest cost. The Midland Railway competed with the L.N.E.R. to get Yorkshire folk to the seaside. Morecambe was the cheaper fare than the fare to Scarborough on the opposite coast. This is an explanation why there are three separate dialects in one town, the fisher folk and the two counties.

Our tribal legends and chronicles tell us the Romans sailed their galleys up the Keer channel to Dockacres which is now four or five miles inland from the open sea.

The Norsemen settled at Heysham, hence the hogsback stone in the churchyard with its curious carvings.

A Spanish galleon is reported to have been wrecked off Heysham port. It was part of the Armada that was chased round the North of Scotland; and survivors came ashore and were absorbed in to the community. Early this century a Spanish iron ore ship was lost in a storm outside Heysham Harbour laden with ore for the Carnforth Iron Works. Two masts and two funnels were visible at low tide for 30 years or so. Age and tradition tells us that St. Patrick was wrecked at Heysham also the small church in the village is called St. Patrick's Chapel.

Then in the 1930's there came the West End Fairground hideous monster known as "Eric the whale". This 60ft monster had a mouth as wide as a hand shrimp net that was lined with rows of 4 inch teeth. When alive, Eric could swish through the ocean with mouth wide open, snap it shut and expel the water and then devour the catch. Eventually Eric was getting a bit "high".

His millionaire Show-Biz owners could not be found, whale steak had not become fashionable on the menu, so Eric went on a one way trip.

Once the funeral smoke of Eric had cleared, we shrimps of Old Poulton (now called Morecambe) could sleep in peace without such fearful nightmares of those teeth. Once more we could echo the town's motto; "Beauty surrounds – health abounds", with just the usual summer rain of crabs and dogfish and the autumn rain of codling, to worry about.

Yes, I enjoyed the Latrobe Federal Band, not forgetting the Devon Bombers Shop Quartet who were making their UK tour debut. I liked their 'McNamara's Band' and 'Down by the Old Mill Stream' in American Style close harmony. The next morning I set my antennae with great care and fine tuning near to Morecambe Town Hall for their Civic Welcome and their concert of reply to the Lady Mayoress and her attendant lady.

I got another good impression of 'Trombones To The Fore', and 'Instant Concert'. This medley of lively tunes with the most unpredictable 'Switches' made me giggle. I really liked their march 'Invercargill' which they used as their stock march of their tour in order to introduce Australian music to the cradle of banding.

To the left of Morecambe Town Hall is a well-preserved stone archway with double doors. This once was the doorway into Poulton Hall, once the home of the Washington family.

The same family of which President George of the United States was a member. Poulton Hall was demolished to make way for a coach park so that more day trippers could come to the seaside and eat fish and chips and then throw scraps off the end of the Old Jetty to us chaps below. But for all that I heard a good rendition of 'Solitaire' that morning.

The Morecambe Silver Band now play this number, and regularly use 'Invergill' as an opening number to their concerts.

The Band and touring party were taken into the Town Hall for coffee and biscuits. (I was very glad not to have been there in the form of shrimp paste in the sandwiches). They all received a brochure and a coloured coat of arms of Lancashire and Morecambe in their new incorporated form. This coat-of-arms includes a shrimp boat under full sail, but where is the shrimp?

Neither was there any reference to the suburb of Bare, once the home of Tiberius, this is where signals were raised to indicate the sands were bare allowing a crossing of the sands to Grange proceed. People do not remember these days – only us shrimps. Phist, they even wrote it up in the Bare Bus shelter that Bare ladies like electric fires. It was placed there by the Electricity Department.

So with that, my story is nearly told, I just floated about after having two such memorable musical treats and gazed at the illuminations each night. It was not long before the British Open Championship band came to Morecambe immediately after their great win at Belle Vue with 'Carnival Romaine' under the baton of Professor Walter Hargreaves. So I wrote up Fairey Aviation Engineering into our long scroll of notable events and hopefully the town will live up to its name and let More Com(b)e."

Acknowledgements

David Joy, for his encouragement and patience.

Jane Keelan, for painstakingly reading through my scribble and making a good job of the typescript.

My son, Paul Nickson, for photographs and the cover picture.

Olive, my wife, for her illustrations.

Jean Sawrey, my sister.

Peter Cherry for kindly letting us use his very good photographs.

My valued assistants: Mike Carter, John Barber, Barry Keelan, John Holland.